*Amber, I pr[...]
opportunity t[...]
Assistant. Wa[...]
in your calli[...] and gifting.*

The Midwife Factor

Spiritual Midwives, More than Babies...

AUDREY MCGRESHAM 12/4/2021

Deliverance
MINISTRY PRESS

Cover design: Star Power | J. Stewart

Interior layout: KUHN Design Group

Library of Congress Control Number: NRC107801

ISBN: 978-1-7367895-0-6

To all the current Spiritual Midwives and up and coming ones. I pray you will freely walk with confidence in your calling, and that God will illuminate the ordered steps He has already prepared for you. As you focus on obedience, follow the directions, prompts, and leadings of the Holy Spirit in providing the assistance needed with spiritual births for Kingdom's growth and God's glory. In the name of Jesus Christ.

His Birthing Assistant,
Audrey

"So God was good to the midwives, and the people multiplied and became very numerous. Since the midwives feared God, He gave them families."

EXODUS 1:20-21 (*HCSB*)

Contents

About the Author 9

Introduction 11

1. Spiritual Midwives 15

2. The Ultimate Coach 23

3. Effective Leadership and Management of
   Spiritual Midwives 37

4. Somebody's Pregnant 47

5. Complications 53

6. Pregnancy Risks 65

7. Delivery 73

8. The Multiplication Factor 85

9. Testimony 103

Scripture Resources 113

Notes 115

About the Author

Audrey McGresham is a gifted teacher and ministry leader. She has served in the roles of ministry chairman, advisor, developer, and missionary. Audrey has a passion for "coming alongside" others and birthing ministries, ideas, and visions of others as they advance the kingdom of God.

Audrey was educated in the Detroit Public Schools system, and after obtaining an associate degree from Highland Park College, she began her teaching career in mathematics. She holds a bachelor's degree from Wayne State University in elementary education, and a master's degree from University of Detroit in high school mathematics. Audrey holds a certificate of completion from the Velma Rosemond School of Prophetic Ministry and accredited six CPE credits from the Chitwood Finances and Tax Service Institute-Church Management and Tax, Minister's & Tax Financial Services. In addition, Audrey is a certified instructor for the National Baptist Convention USA, Inc.

Sister McGresham currently serves as the Adult Department Sunday School Superintendent at Tabernacle Missionary Baptist Church, in Detroit, Michigan. She is an active member of the Women and Girls' Ministry, Media Ministry, Teaching Ministry, and Virtual Tech Team. Additionally, during her forty plus years as a member, Sister Audrey has served in many other areas of ministry, including advisor and chairman of the Women & Girls' Ministry and Steering Committee, lead coordinator of the Commissions on Ministries, a participant in the mission work of Tabernacle in "Reclaiming Our Jerusalem" and the "Family Islands" of the Bahamas, a delegate at the National Baptist Congress of Christian Education, and Christ's Coordinators Ministry Organization Team. In her spare time, Audrey loves spending time with her adult children and grandchildren.

Introduction

"There are generations yet unborn, whose very lives will be shifted and shaped by the moves you make and the actions you take."

ANDY ANDREWS

In August 1994, while participating in the Bahamian Fellowship with members of my church, Tabernacle Missionary Baptist Church of Detroit, MI., I waded in the Atlantic Ocean as I waited for the sunrise early one morning. The Lord spoke to me in my spirit and said, "I am calling you to the Ministry of Deliverance." Eager to serve the Lord and be obedient, I bought every book I could on exorcism and demon possession. I readied myself for the worst of the worst. All I could picture in my mind was the priest sweating, choking, and calling out demons in the 1973 horror film, *The Exorcist*. I was willing to roll with it, but I was sure I had signed up for more than I bargained! It turned out that God's idea of me being a deliverer didn't have anything to do with the priest in the film.

It wasn't until August of the year 1998 that the Lord announced, in my spirit, "It is time." I didn't know at the time what this would entail, how it would fit, or even that it actually had a connection to the 1994 call, until driving home from a meeting of the Growth Commission in November. The Holy Spirit reminded me of Proverbs 3:5. It was during that drive that the understanding of the 1994 CALL became more defined. My initial understanding had been limited to a focus of releasing individuals from demonic strongholds, oppression, guilt, unforgiveness, etc. But as I continued to receive instruction about spiritual midwifery and spiritual births, I began to embrace the vision for the body of Christ. The vision was to deliver and birth by setting free the gifts, the visions, the dreams, and the spiritual power that is developing within us so that it may mature [see Ephesians 4] and serve the body of Christ and glorify the Father.

Ever ready to work in His kingdom, I dove in headfirst and have since continued to be a spiritual midwife to those who are called to work for His glory. It hasn't always been smiles and good times either. Like any ministry, spiritual midwifing has its own set of challenges. It can be difficult to walk away from something you've helped build from the ground up, only to have to do it all over again with the next ministry. Sleepless nights are often a work hazard, as I labor to bring forth someone else's vision and stand in the gap for them when they run out of steam. And let's face it, sometimes it's a thankless ministry. But when I am reminded that my "why" is rooted in my desire to put a smile on God's face, I am able to love my calling and enjoy the fruition of dreams. I behold the seeds I've planted and sown and thank God for giving me the opportunity to serve Him in this great work!

The body of Christ has the need for spiritual midwives to assist in the birthing of God's visions and dreams. God has impregnated His people with promises, possibilities, potential, purposes, and power. Some have been carrying visions and dreams for years, while others are ready to deliver. Utilizing effective church leadership and management, the Pastor and/or leaders must come to understand the role, the reason, the risk, the resistance, and the results of The Midwife Factor. A remnant of spiritual midwives is waiting to do what God has directed them to do in the deliverance of the spiritual births of His people during and after the birthing.

I have been called and assigned to function as a spiritual midwife in the ministry of deliverance. I thought when called to the ministry of deliverance it was to deliver those in bondage from the enemy, but my spirit rehearsed during that time the thought that I wanted to be so intimate with God that I will know His "heartbeat" concerning matters. I was given clarity as I was reminded "not to lean to my own understanding." The deliverance I would be involved in was and is in the assisting of growth, development, and support prior to and during a time of spiritual births. It also would include, when necessary, help with the afterbirth of going forth and multiplying.

I, Audrey McGresham, am a vessel of God whom He uses with the word of knowledge, word of wisdom, and discernment to encourage, equip, and edify His people as they fulfill His directive to "... Be fruitful, and multiply, and replenish the earth, and subdue it." I serve as one of the spiritual midwives in the deliverance ministry, as HIS Birthing Assistant.

Are you looking for a promise of God to be fulfilled in your life or in the lives of your loved ones—whether it is healing, rest, salvation, peace, or wisdom? Are you waiting for a vision, a work of ministry, or a dream God has given you to manifest? Or maybe you are reading this book with much anticipation of the power of God to be demonstrated in a specific area of your life. If any of these questions ring true for you, you are in need of THE MIDWIFE FACTOR.

Spiritual Midwives

Who are They?

According to Webster's Dictionary, a midwife is one that helps to produce or bring forth something.[1] With this definition in mind, anyone in the kingdom of God—male or female—can be a *spiritual* midwife. "There is no longer Jew or Gentile, slave or free, nor male and female. For you are all one in Christ Jesus" (Galatians 3:28). When I finally received an understanding of this spiritual role, which is to assist in the spiritual births of the Kingdom, I could more readily draw parallels between it and the role of a midwife who assists with childbirth in the natural realm.

DISCERN, DEVELOP, DEMONSTRATE, AND DELIVER

I believe, The Midwife Factor is applied and operates in one's sphere of influence to allow life and to deliver multiplication for the Kingdom's Sake and God's Glory (see Exodus 1:17, *HCSB*, "... let the boys live"). A spiritual midwife is one who discerns the gifts, talents, abilities, passions, visions, etc. that God has placed in individuals. His birthing assistant is one who is willing to help birth, deliver, and bring forth the things of God from individuals. The spiritual midwife and His birthing assistants are activated to discern, develop, demonstrate, and deliver; they help others see their potential and embrace their passions to accomplish tasks and provide support and resources that are beneficial to the growth and development of God's people.

God also provides gifts, talents, visions, etc. through various people who may be in areas outside of traditional ministry. (Note: These people are not just reserved for ministry and "church stuff;" hence, the "More than Babies" that highlights additional ways God brings forth His masterpieces). Ephesians 2:10 reminds us that, "We are God's masterpiece. He has created us anew in Christ Jesus, so that we can do the good things He planned for us long ago."

"More than Babies" presents opportunities for God's children to shine their light and apply the salt needed in the earth as they discern, develop, demonstrate, and deliver what God has placed within individuals and still emulating God's love to non-believers and pointing them to His Son, Jesus Christ while offering hope and encouragement to their sisters and brothers in Christ Jesus, making an impact on others for the Kingdom's sake and God's glory.

A spiritual midwife can assist an individual or a collective birthing of babies as God has ordained. God has ordained. This can include churches, ministries, projects, dreams, visions, and businesses that advance the Kingdom of God. Spiritual midwives can also help in the discipling and mentoring of other Christians. According to Margaret Gunther, author of the article "A Spiritual Midwife: God's Helpers in Birthing New Life"

> We need to nurture further gifted people in the body who direct us. We need to pay attention to the people and resources we have already been given. We want to provide

everyone with good opportunities to go deep. It will take more spiritual midwives — men or women who can help with the spiritual birthing process. We need them, whoever they might be.[2]

Spiritual midwives play important roles in the Kingdom. They may go unnoticed or may not have a ministry title such as pastor, teacher, or ministry leader. But nevertheless, they are often working behind the scenes to assist God in bringing new life where it's needed.

THE ROLE OF SPIRITUAL MIDWIVES

Spiritual midwives are both male and female with the assignment to assist with the deliverance of spiritual births. They work to assist and provide a healthy birthing atmosphere before, during, and even after the birth. The role of a spiritual midwife is to encourage, enlighten, exhort, edify, warn, guide, direct, comfort and console the birther as well as collect any equipment necessary for the birthing process. I used to find myself in meetings and in other places I didn't plan to be initially. Later, I would come to realize that help was needed to encourage further development of a spiritual pregnancy.

I have had individuals to tell me things like, "You are always around doing something," or "You are at just about in every meeting I go to. Is there anything you are not a part of?" Sometimes people have even suggested that I had no business being where I was or doing what I was doing. I used to take offense to these types of comments before I began to understand the role of a spiritual midwife during the embryo stage of a ministry or project.

Just like in the natural realm, we can't always predict when the time is right for the birthing process to begin. A spiritual midwife can be called upon at any time. When there is a threat of miscarriage, the spiritual midwife relieves the pregnant one from factors that cause stress or undo pressure. In other words, the spiritual midwife does anything to help bring the pregnancy to full-term.

THE NEED FOR SPIRITUAL MIDWIVES

The need for spiritual midwives in our churches and ministries is evidenced by the problems faced in our society. Churches should be change agents in their surrounding communities, but change begins with the people of God operating in the power God has given. In his article, "Honorable Men Seek Spiritual Midwives," Gillis Triplet outlines reasons why spiritual midwives are needed in today's churches:

> That is the problem with many of our modern day churches. They have the numbers in terms of head count, but they don't wax mighty in their community, city, state or nation. These churches make a lot of noise, but they don't show forth the awesome power of God by empowering the poor, mending the brokenhearted, setting the captives free or healing the sick.
>
> In this next move of God, the people will not only increase in numbers, but they will wax mighty in the Word of God and in the anointing of the Holy Spirit (see Acts 6:7). Through their hands God will wrought mighty miracles of healing, provision, restoration and renewal (see John 3:21).[3]

STANDING IN THE GAP

To prevent the person with the dream or vision from aborting, the spiritual midwife may step in and carry the spiritual child for a period of time in order to allow the impregnated person to be strengthened or even realize that they are pregnant. A Sunday school teacher once told me that teaching was not what he was called to do; he was just standing in the gap until the one who had been called accepted his or her call.

At times, spiritual midwives can be found standing in the gap. However, they must realize that by standing in the gap, they are not the one that has been called to "fill" the gap. Like the Sunday school teacher, one is sometimes positioned to carry out tasks as they wait for the one God has called. When standing in the gap, spiritual midwives must be ready to relinquish the position once the person who is called surfaces. The transition can be seamless when both the midwife and the one God has called allow the Holy Spirit to govern their thinking and actions during the process.

There are times when the spiritual midwife has to help individuals recognize that they are the one that will fit and fill every nook and cranny. Unlike what happens when standing in the gap, one filling the gap leaves no area uncovered.

The Spiritual Midwife is a role exercising a ministry of helps, where one may find herself or himself among "top officials" or just among the "down home folks." Either way, the plan is that the spiritual midwife ministers to the one with the vision—the one that has been impregnated by God Himself. This form of leadership provides help in any and every way possible to work toward the birthing of that ministry. A spiritual midwife's role is vital to Kingdom building.

THE MIDWIFE FACTOR MEDITATION

- *A spiritual midwife is one called to assist with spiritual births that advance the Kingdom of God.*

- *The Kingdom births can include churches, ministries, projects, dreams, visions, and businesses.*

- *The role of a spiritual midwife is to exhort, encourage, edify, comfort, console, guide, and direct spiritual births.*

- *A spiritual midwife may need to step in and prevent a dream or vision from aborting.*

THE MIDWIFE FACTOR
ESSENTIAL CARE REFLECTION

1. When you reflect on the definition of a spiritual midwife, how do you see yourself operating in this role?

2. What qualities do you feel you possess that align with the role of a spiritual midwife?

3. What is your immediate response when a spiritual project/ministry is underway or when the groundwork is being laid for a new ministry? Do you find yourself jumping in and assisting? Do others count on you to help get things done in various ministries?

4. How do people you know fit the definition and role of a spiritual midwife?

2

The Ultimate Coach

Responding to the Spiritual Midwife Calling

"What you are is God's gift to you.
What you make of yourself is your gift to God."

ANONYMOUS

As you ponder the thought of responding to the call of a spiritual midwife—the ultimate coach—perhaps you are concerned with your life's journey. Maybe you are considering all the issues, challenges, and possible drama you may face, or maybe you simply have doubts about who you are in Christ. Is there some deep insecurity that plagues you? Are you hindered by past failures, filled with guilt about the times you didn't represent the Lord righteously? Your thought life may be creating a spiritual barrier that is preventing you from accepting your calling.

Jesus, the Real Ultimate Coach, encourages us through the writer of Proverbs 24. Verse 16 states, "The godly may trip seven times, but they will get up again. But one disaster is enough to overthrow the wicked." So, for every time you have fallen due to issues, circumstances, drama, and attacks that you have encountered, know that you have experienced God's stand-up power, and He has given you the ability to *keep* getting up.

My sister, my brother, your faith, trust, and relationship with Jesus Christ position you to receive a gift of grace from God—righteousness.

23

It is because of this gift that all those times you have fallen, either because of your decisions or at the hands or plots of others, you have been able to stand again. Pastor Nathan Johnson shared in his lesson, "The Resiliency of the Righteous," that because of salvation, "You have God living in you who strengthens you who will give you standing up power when life would knock you down."[1] Your testimony of God's power to lift you and help you stand again will provide encouragement to those around you.

THE MINISTRY OF HELPS

Your calling as a spiritual midwife is a part of the ministry of helps. Paul identified helps as a spiritual gift in 1 Corinthians 12:28, *HCSB*, "And God has placed these in the church: first apostles, second prophets, third teachers, next miracles, then gifts of healing, helping, managing, various kinds of languages." In his lesson on the Helps Ministry, Pastor Christopher McMichael, of Engrafted Word Church, puts it this way: "Because God has set helps as an office in the church, it must by nature, be a supernatural position. Helps can be defined as a supernaturally endowed office to work in and advance the kingdom of God. The ministry of helps is EVERY Christian's calling. We are all called to help propel the gospel of Jesus Christ. Christianity is not a spectatorship."[2] We can understand from Scripture that all believers are called to help others. However, because helps is a gift of the Holy Spirit, spiritual midwives and others endowed with this gift may have much more of a capacity to help than other believers, as they possess a supernatural capacity to provide assistance.

The ministry of helps can support others who are hurting or experiencing difficult times or assist in more practical ways as stated in the article, "The Spiritual Gift of Helps—What is It?" "The needs may be more practical in nature. Helping may be related to providing assistance in a way as to enable another to accomplish their ministry task. Or the needs may be more spiritual in nature; a helper would provide others with encouragement or discernment or the like."[3]

When we help others, we not only demonstrate God's love for

mankind, but His ability to provide healing, forgiveness, restoration, reconciliation, and wholeness in each of our lives. Our submission and willingness to be used by God enables us to develop a more intimate relationship with Him, positioning us to experience the true grace of God as is given in 1 Peter 5—to be restored, established, and strengthened by God Himself. A spiritual midwife is not a spectator, but an engaged participant in the body of Christ. We serve God first and foremost. We are not volunteers for ministry; we are servants of the Most High God. McMichael describes the differences between servanthood and volunteerism in his comparison chart
"What Helps is Not."[4]

Table 1: What Helps Is Not!

Helps is not being a volunteer! Helps is ministry servant-hood.[5]

→ Servants serve at the Master's behest.	→ Volunteers can quit any time they want.
→ Servants look for rewards in heaven.	→ Volunteers look to be paid in accolades, praise, and thanks.
→ Servants seek what's best for the church.	→ Volunteers seek what's best for them.
→ Servants live for the Kingdom of God.	→ Volunteers flirt with the Kingdom.
→ Helps is not you doing the pastor a favor.	→ The pastor is actually doing you a favor by letting you help him by serving in his church.
→ Helps is not the place to do a mediocre job.	→ If a paycheck would motivate you to do a better job for the kingdom, then you are a hireling.

Table 1: What Helps is Not. Adapted from Source: J. Christopher McMichael, "Helps Ministry, Lesson 1 Part 1"

As McMichael points out, there is a vast difference between servanthood and volunteerism. We must adjust our attitudes accordingly. Unlike volunteers, we can't just quit (at least we shouldn't) when we don't feel rewarded or acknowledged or when we don't get our way. Christian author and personal growth coach, Sherrhonda Denice, who is also a fellow spiritual midwife, puts it this way when asked about her role as a servant for Christ, "I don't seek recognition for anything I do at church or for ministry. I am content with stapling papers or sealing envelopes if that's what needs to be done. I don't care who acknowledges me. As long as God smiles, that's all that matters. A million people can applaud you, but if God isn't happy with you, nothing else matters."[6]

Like Denice, it is imperative that spiritual midwives adopt a spirit of "doing what needs to be done." This is our role. It's our job description. It's our mantra. It's our mission. Ministry work is hardly ever pretty or glamourous, and it may not always be rewarding or satisfying. But hey, newsflash: We are working for God! Can't you just see the God of the Universe smiling about the humble way you avail yourself to Him without desiring anything but a "well done" from Him? No cameras. No autographs. No paparazzi. Just God smiling because of little ole you. Doesn't that feel wonderful? I don't know about you, but the thought of God smiling because of me is more gratifying than anything else I can imagine.

PREPARATION OF A SPIRITUAL MIDWIFE

One of the first assignments I was entrusted with as a spiritual midwife was assisting one of my former church ministers, Rev. Dr. Grace Moorman, with planning a women's conference. I bet you would love to know what my exciting role was. Well, hold on to your seat, it was super glamorous. No. I'm just kidding. It wasn't glamourous at all. It was super simple. Proofreading. Yep. That's right. Proof. Reading. That was my assignment—to proofread and make sure the literature, handouts, and packets that the attendees would receive contained correct grammar and punctuation and were free of typos. And you know what?

I did it with diligence and excellence because I realized even then that God had called me to support the conference, and I needed to be willing to work in any capacity necessary. So, that's what I did.

Your preparation begins with your willingness to serve. This is the beginning of your training as a spiritual midwife. Spiritual Midwifing 101. Chere Nabor, founder of Women of the Root, a women's support ministry, is experienced in assisting others to walk in their calling. She says, "God is sovereign! And as we seek to operate in the call that He has placed on our lives we must prepare ourselves as willing vessels."[7]

If we view ourselves from the lens of the Master, as vessels to be used, servanthood should come quite naturally. Nabor states that she prepares to meet the goals of her ministry by engaging in "continued development (spiritual and natural) through immersion in God's word to provide revelation and to sustain me, prayer and meditation as a means of restoration, mentoring as a learning process to both teach and learn, and professional study and certificates...."[8]

But just because you may be spiritually gifted, doesn't mean you don't need training. As you lean on God for guidance in your spiritual and business/ministry affairs, professional study and training are necessary tools you can't afford to neglect. They increase your knowledge of the innerworkings of the ministries/businesses you support, help you to sharpen your present skills, as well as develop new ones that are valuable for the tasks at hand and future assignments. Training is a win-win component of the spiritual midwife development process.

Take my first spiritual midwife assignment as a proofreader for example. It may seem like a menial task to some, but it has been instrumental in increasing my skill level as a proofreader. It was on-the-job training! Now, some may think "Oh that is so boring!" And others may envision themselves speaking at conferences instead of sitting at a desk or table someplace proofreading. However, let me ask you a question: Have you ever received materials at a conference or workshop that were subpar? Unprofessional? Riddled with errors? I have! And it can really detract from presentations. This should never be the case with Believers because we work for the Master!

Everything we do needs to be done with excellence. As I became more and more engaged in ministry and willing to do whatever tasks were necessary, God was slowly increasing my skill level. I am confident and proficient in crafting materials for workshops and conferences. I am skilled at planning conferences for hundreds or even thousands of people. Each time I supported, I was learning from and being trained by women and men who had experience in the area I was serving in at the time. Nowadays, I teach at conferences and workshops. Those proofreading skills have never gone out of style nor has any of the other skills I've learned over the years: scheduling speakers, making hotel reservations and other accommodations for attendees, and selecting workshop sites. All these skills have been used by God to bless me and others!

We must learn to bloom where we are planted. Don't look for assignments that will "put you in front of the cameras." Look to be used by God. He will advance you when the time is right.

PROFESSIONAL STUDY

In addition to sharpening skills from on-the-job training, we must also seek to develop professional skills via professional study. What I mean by this is making it a practice to take structured classes or workshops that will make you more proficient in serving. For example, technology is ever changing, and as we have adapted to our "new normal" of working and learning online due to the pandemic, we must be able to navigate these spaces with competence and use different methods of technology to continue to promote the Gospel, and disciple others.

Many churches are now holding worship services and other meetings online. Anyone who is serving in ministry needs to be familiar with the tools needed to continue to do what we have been called by Christ to do. That may include taking a class on how to use Zoom effectively, how to engage on social media, or how to develop multimedia PowerPoints. These are necessary skills for the present time and the future.

Spiritual midwives need to remain at the forefront of learning. It would be near impossible to support someone using the present technology platforms for meeting and engaging others if you are not adequately prepared through proper training. God has given you the ability to learn and synthesize information so that you can carry out your mission. I stated earlier that you've got to be ready to serve in whatever capacity you're needed, but this may require more than on-the-job training.

Making sure meetings go smoothly may entail becoming well versed with Robert's Rules of Order by attending a class or training. Similarly, you may need to attend a class or workshop on ministry finance, or how to aid people in crisis if your church or ministry has a hotline number for people to call for help or assistance. It is the spiritual midwife's responsibility to make him/herself as prepared as possible to serve and support.

SOFT SKILLS

The ability to listen, communicate, adapt, and work well within a team, can increase a spiritual midwife's ability to support others. In the business world, they call these soft skills. However, some of us may remember our parents referring to them as "people skills." According to TheBalanceCareers.com, a career development website, "Soft skills are non-technical skills that relate to how you work. They include how you interact with colleagues, how you solve problems, and how you manage your work."[9] These skills can include but are not limited to communication skills, listening skills, the ability to work in groups or teams, adaptability, and demonstrate emotional intelligence by learning to read/recognize and respond appropriately to their own as well as others' body language and emotions. These are all necessary skills needed for working with others.

Team building activities are a great way for ministry workers to get to know each other better and gain experience with diverse personalities and work styles. Soft skills such as improving communication or listening can be taught during team building activities at ministry retreats or trainings by someone who is skilled in this area. I once heard a minister ask the question: "Do you ever wonder why God gave us one mouth and two ears?" We can only guess that the Lord wants us to listen more than we speak! These sorts of skills can improve how we as spiritual midwives work with others as we allow the Holy Spirit to give us wisdom to apply our knowledge. And above all, He has given us the fruit of the Spirit. "But the fruit of the Spirit is love, joy, peace, patience, kindness, goodness, faith, gentleness, self-control. Against such things there is no law" (Galatians 5:22-23, *HCSB*). You cannot go wrong with these!

PATH OF THE SPIRITUAL MIDWIFE

The path of the spiritual midwife is one that is carefully aligned with God's visions and goals. As you present yourself as an instrument to be used, you will be more in tune with what God speaks to you and what direction He wants you to move in, so that you are not needlessly spending time on projects, ministry, and other support roles God has not assigned you.

Most people tend to think that when they do any sort of ministry work, they are doing a "good work." But what if God hasn't called them to it? Sometimes in churches and ministry, we are so quick to fill "positions" or get help that we don't pay attention to people's gifts or the lack thereof when asking people to serve. Since we want to work with excellence, we need to pray and be certain that God is calling us to be involved in various ministries. Yes, He wants us to serve. Therefore, we need to be properly placed. Spiritual midwives may *personally* feel compelled to assist in some situations, but we want to always be in alignment with what God wants. God has a perfect plan for how He wants to use us; we need to stick close enough to Him to hear His instructions and follow them. I call this the Spiritual Midwife Path.

Path #1

→ **Walk in partnership with Christ.**

> *The Spirit of the Sovereign Lord is upon me, for the Lord has anointed me to bring good news to the poor. He has sent me to comfort the brokenhearted and to proclaim that*

captives will be released and prisoners will be freed. He has sent me to tell those who mourn that the time of the Lord's favor has come, and with it, the day of God's anger against their enemies to all who mourn in Israel, he will give a crown of beauty for ashes, a joyous blessing instead of mourning, festive praise instead of despair. In their righteousness, they will be like great oaks that the Lord has planted for his own glory (Isaiah 61:1-3).

Path # 2

→ **Walk worthy of your calling.**

Therefore I, a prisoner for serving the Lord, beg you to lead a life worthy of your calling, for you have been called by God. Always be humble and gentle. Be patient with each other, making allowance for each other's faults because of your love. Make every effort to keep yourselves united in the Spirit, binding yourselves together with peace (Ephesians 4:1-3).

Path #3

→ **Walk in the gifts found in the Church.**

Now these are the gifts Christ gave to the church: the apostles, the prophets, the evangelists, and the pastors and teachers (Ephesians 4:11).

Path #4

→ **Walk in participation in the body of Christ.**

Their responsibility is to equip God's people to do his work and build up the church, the body of Christ. This will continue until we all come to such unity in our faith and knowledge of God's Son that we will be mature in the Lord, measuring up to the full and complete standard of Christ (Ephesians 4:12-13).

Path # 5

→ **Walk in patience as you embrace your calling and run the race.**

> *Therefore, since we are surrounded by such a huge crowd of witnesses to the life of faith, let us strip off every weight that slows us down, especially the sin that so easily trips us up. And let us run with endurance the race God has set before us. We do this by keeping our eyes on Jesus, the champion who initiates and perfects our faith. Because of the joy awaiting him, he endured the cross, disregarding its shame. Now he is seated in the place of honor beside God's throne (Hebrews 12:1-2).*

Path #6

→ **Walk in witness of the fruit produced as you follow Christ.**

> *Jesus came and told his disciples, "I have been given all authority in heaven and on earth. Therefore, go and make disciples of all the nations, baptizing them in the name of the Father and the Son and the Holy Spirit. Teach these new disciples to obey all the commands I have given you. And be sure of this: I am with you always, even to the end of the age" (Matthew 28:18-20).*

Path #7

→ **Walk in God's Peace.**

> *Then you will experience God's peace, which exceeds anything we can understand. His peace will guard your hearts and minds as you live in Christ Jesus (Philippians 4:7).*

As you consider the path of the spiritual midwife, review the "path" Scriptures, and meditate on them daily as you serve.

TIMING OF THE SPIRITUAL MIDWIFE

So now you've got your marching orders. You know what preparation is needed. You know what path to take. But what about timing? The natural birthing process is full of necessary periods of transitions, nausea, adjustments, struggles, pain, and even transformation! These events occur at various times in the spiritual birthing process as well. Therefore, as a spiritual midwife, you must recognize that timing will be a key element in the support you lend to others. When a spiritual pregnancy develops (a new ministry, project, or business that will advance the Kingdom) like a good ole Double Dutch jump rope pro, you've got to know when to jump in and when to jump out.

Your support may be needed to get the train moving, and then another spiritual midwife may be needed to get the train to the next stop. A spiritual midwife must be sensitive to the move of the Spirit and sensitive to God's timing. Even when given an idea from God, timing will be an important part of how the spiritual birth comes to fruition. We can't take it personally if we present ideas that are not readily accepted or rejected totally.

God has perfect timing, so we must lean into it with submission. For example, at my church, we are welcome to share our ideas about new ministries or about how an existing ministry or it's processes can be improved. However, a lot of times, my pastor will say, "Let me pray on that," or "Let me think about it some more." An eager spiritual midwife might take these statements as a "no" and feel frustrated. But most times, it boils down to timing. God doesn't always reveal His plans in the manner we may desire. We've got to stay on the Spiritual Midwife Path and keep our spiritual ears open.

Wrong timing can sabotage plans. Spiritual midwives must remember the warning in John 10:10, "The thief's purpose is to steal and kill and destroy. My purpose is to give them a rich and satisfying life." Only the enemy is out to steal, kill, and destroy. In contrast, our Lord wants to bless us. He wants to bless the works of our hands. We must trust Him to do the work He's called us to do by letting Him work through us. Getting out of sync with Him can lead to devastating consequences. Operating in alignment with God is realizing that the *Kairos* moment

of birth is in His hands! And in the '9th month' of God's timing birthing occurs. Birth will come … wait for it!

The Real Ultimate Coach has recorded in His Word reminders for
us to wait on the right timing that only He sets. In Psalm 27:13-14 it
states, "Yet I am confident I will see the Lord's goodness while I am here
in the land of the living. Wait patiently for the Lord. Be brave and cou-
rageous. Yes, wait patiently for the Lord." Reverence and Fear of the
Lord help His birthing assistants and spiritual midwives of God and
give them instructions concerning the new birth as they respond to the
directions of the Holy Spirit. As you respond to your call by acknowl-
edging the Word of God, He will provide you with the plans determin-
ing the new birth, what is needed to accompany the birth, and how to
navigate the birthing process.

- *Don't allow personal insecurities or past failures to prevent you from accepting your call as a spiritual midwife.*

- *Your relationship with Christ positions you to receive a gift of grace from God. This enables you to stand after any "fall."*

- *Your preparation as a spiritual midwife begins with your willingness to serve in any capacity necessary.*

- *Spiritual midwives should be engaged participants in the body of Christ.*

- *Spiritual midwives must engage in professional study and training to help them work for God with excellence.*

THE MIDWIFE FACTOR
ESSENTIAL CARE REFLECTION

1. What personal failures or insecurities may be preventing you from accepting your call as a spiritual midwife?

2. What are your feelings about being able and ready to "do whatever is necessary" for the work of the Kingdom?

3. On the Spiritual Midwife Path, which path number do you operate in most confidently? Which of the path Scriptures speak to you the most?

4. What gifts and/or skills do you presently possess? How have you been using them in ministry? If you have not been using them, explain why not. What would help or encourage you to utilize your gifts and skills more?

5. Talk about an experience/situation where timing played a key role. Did you feel you operated within God's timing or outside of it? What did you learn from your experience?

3

Effective Leadership and Management of Spiritual Midwives

Spot the Spiritual Midwives, Beware of the Pharaohs

"We must learn to see the God-print on each human being."
PASTOR NATHAN JOHNSON

SPOTTING SPIRITUAL MIDWIVES

Effective church leaders and good stewards in the management of the church must identify the spiritual midwives within their congregations, as well as the pharaohs that are operating within and outside of their people. How do you "spot" the spiritual midwives? I'm glad you asked!

One of the first ways these midwives can be recognized is by their FEAR OF GOD. The choice to operate in the fear of the Lord produces fruit others will be able to witness. Look for individuals that demonstrate evidence that they fear the Lord. Let me share with you some of the blessings those who fear God will receive:

Psalm 128:1	*How joyful are those <u>who fear the LORD</u>— all who follow his ways!*
Psalm 128:2	*You will enjoy the fruit of your labor. How joyful and prosperous you will be!*
Psalm 111:10	*<u>Fear of the Lord</u> is the foundation of true wisdom. All who obey his commandments will grow in wisdom. Praise him forever!*
Psalm 111:5	*He gives food to those who <u>fear him</u>; he always remembers his covenant.*
Psalm 103:17	*But the love of the Lord remains forever with those who fear him. His salvation extends to the children's children …*
Proverbs 1:7	*<u>Fear of the Lord</u> is the foundation of true knowledge …*
Proverbs 2:5	*Then you will understand what it means to <u>fear the Lord</u>, and you will gain knowledge of God.*
Proverbs 2:6	*For the Lord grants wisdom! From his mouth come knowledge and understanding.*
Proverbs 8:13	*All who <u>fear the Lord</u> will hate evil…*
Proverbs 10:27	*<u>Fear of the Lord</u> lengthens one's life…*
Proverbs 14:27	*<u>Fear of the Lord</u> is a life-giving fountain; it offers escape from the snares of death.*
Proverbs 15:33	*<u>Fear of the Lord</u> teaches wisdom; humility precedes honor.*
Proverbs 16:6	*Unfailing love and faithfulness make atonement for sin. By <u>fearing the Lord</u>, people avoid evil.*
Proverbs 19:23	*<u>Fear of the Lord</u> leads to life, bringing security and protection from harm.*

Proverbs 22:4   *True humility and <u>fear of the Lord</u> lead to riches, honor, and long life.*

RECOGNIZING THE MIDWIFE FACTORS

Another way to spot spiritual midwives is to recognize the midwife factors. We can find some of these in Exodus 1:15-22, *KJV*.

- **Kings and top officials speak to them.**

  15 And the king of Egypt spake to the Hebrew midwives…

- **Their names mean fair.**

  15 …of which the name of the one was Shiphrah…

- **Their names mean splendid from an unused root/ meaning to glitter.**

  15 …and the name of the other Puah:

- **They are in a position of authority, duty, or trust given to a person, as in a government or corporation: the office of vice president. The administrative personnel, executives, or staff.**

  16 And he said, When ye do the office of a midwife…

- **They see.**

  16 …to the Hebrew women, and see them upon the stool; if it be a son, then ye shall kill him: but if it be a daughter, then she shall live.

- **They fear God and "save."**

  17 But the midwives feared God, and did not as the king of Egypt commanded them, but saved the men children alive.

- **They are called by Kings and summoned to high places.**

  [18] And the king of Egypt called for the midwives,…

- **They speak to leaders/those in authority.**

  [18] *and said unto them, Why have ye done this thing, and have saved the men children alive?* [19] *And the midwives said unto Pharaoh…*

- **They understand and can communicate that God can and will operate without their assistance.** (As my Pastor, Nathan Johnson, always says, "God has options we don't have!")

  [19]…*Because the Hebrew women are not as the Egyptian women; for they are lively, and are delivered ere the midwives come in unto them.*

- **Their fear (reverence) of God and their obedience to God pleases Him, therefore He blesses them and provides for them.**

  [20] *Therefore God dealt well with the midwives: and the people multiplied, and waxed very mighty.* [21] *And it came to pass, because the midwives feared God, that he made them houses.*

- **Their obedience to God angers the enemy.**

  [22] And Pharaoh charged all his people, saying, Every son that is born ye shall cast into the river, and every daughter ye shall save alive.

LOOK FOR THE FRUIT

Spiritual midwives who are in alignment with God will demonstrate the character of God and will produce the fruit of the Spirit we discussed in Chapter 2. So, you need to look for the fruit! I promise you won't have to look too hard. Do you recognize people in your church congregation or ministry who operate in love and have a willing spirit to help others, often without being asked? Are there people in your church congregation or ministry who are adept at handling small, seemingly menial tasks that are vital to the ministry? Do you observe those who are skilled at helping others to start new ministries or who are skilled at helping others to birth dreams and visions? These people might be spiritual midwives sitting right under your nose.

What's the big deal? Why is it so important to recognize the spiritual midwives among us? Well, you see, spiritual midwives who are undergirding others and helping to bring dreams and visions to life are helping to sustain and grow ministries. Most of all, they are assisting in promoting the Gospel message and turning people to Christ. That's the bottom line. It's all for the glory of God. It's a chain reaction that will impact the local community and the world at large. The vision God gives His people is instrumental in bringing forth fruit—the multiplication factor. There is a danger of not knowing who or what your resources are. It can lead to stagnation instead of multiplication! As Pastor Hein van Wyk, Co-founder of Sharefaith.com states,

> Many leaders are simply titular placeholders. They hold a job, make some decisions, but they don't advance their organizations. Why not? Simply put, they lack vision. You serve a big God. In fact, he's bigger than you can possibly imagine. So go ahead and dream. Cast your vision, and live it out. If you don't have a vision, you can still be a leader, but you're not going to go anywhere.[1]

Proverbs 29: 18 *KJV* reminds us that *where there is no vision people perish*. Spiritual midwives can help leaders to understand and/or develop visions for ministries and help them to execute the visions the way God intended. In addition, spiritual midwives may even share their own visions God has placed in their hearts. These visions are spiritual pregnancies that need attention. As spiritual midwives assist others, they need support as well to fend off the attacks of the enemy that interfere with the birthing process and can cause spontaneous or deliberate attempts to abort.

LOOKOUT FOR PHARAOHS

Now that we know how to recognize the spiritual midwives, we must realize that the enemy does not wish for God's people to grow and advance in Him. We know that the people of God are pregnant with promises, possibilities, potentials, purposes, and power, and many are ready to deliver. But where there are spiritual midwives, the pharaohs won't be too far away. Therefore, pastors and leaders must beware. There are those who have assigned themselves (as Pharaoh did in Moses' time) to be the ones to determine what positions and opportunities they will allow the people of God to attain based on their own judgment of people's worth or what they believe the people of God need or are entitled to.

These self-assigned pharaohs' attempts to destroy parts of the ministry, eliminate certain populations from the church, and impede the multiplication/growth or advancement of a congregation in the Kingdom of God are due to their own fears of inadequacies, misunderstandings, and a lack of knowledge of who they are in Christ and/or who spiritual midwives are in Christ. Let's take a closer look at Exodus 1:15-22, *NIV*.

> The king of Egypt said to the Hebrew midwives, whose names were Shiphrah and Puah, "When you are helping the Hebrew women during childbirth on the delivery stool, if you see that the baby is a boy, kill him; but if it is a girl, let her live." The midwives, however, feared God and did not do what the king of Egypt had told them to do; they let the boys live. Then the king of Egypt summoned the midwives and asked them, "Why have you done this? Why have you let the boys live?" The midwives answered Pharaoh, "Hebrew women are not like Egyptian women; they are vigorous and give birth before the midwives arrive." So

God was kind to the midwives and the people increased
and became even more numerous. And because the midwives feared God, he gave them families of their own. Then
Pharaoh gave this order to all his people: "Every Hebrew
boy that is born you must throw into the Nile, but let every
girl live" (Exodus 1:15-22, NIV).

Notice in Exodus 1:16, *NIV*, the directive was given to destroy
the male children—a calculated effort to control the population of a
people, only went to two midwives, Shiphrah and Puah. Because of
their fear of the Lord and their willingness to be a birthing assistant of
God, increase (what I call the midwife factor multiplication) occurred
among the Israelites. The word of God states in Exodus 1:20, *NIV*, "…
the people increased and became even more numerous." Then in verse
22 of the same chapter, Pharaoh gives the "order to all his people" to
throw every boy that is born into the Nile.

As you can see, pharaohs will make attempts to call some spiritual
midwives aside and give them destructive directions that are contrary
to the will of God. Some who function as pharaohs will even create
situations in which they misuse their power and place the people in
oppressed positions due to their own fears and insecurities. Others are
novices that have come into power not realizing the history of God and
His people. As a leader it's up to you to be on the lookout.

THE MIDWIFE FACTOR MEDITATION

- *One of the ways to spot spiritual midwives is their fear of God.*

- *Spiritual midwives can be recognized by the midwife factors.*

- *Effective leadership and management of spiritual midwives will lead to the multiplication factor.*

- *Pharaohs in churches and ministries can hinder the spiritual birthing process.*

THE MIDWIFE FACTOR
ESSENTIAL CARE REFLECTION

1. How easy or difficult do you think it is to spot spiritual midwives and lookout for pharaohs in the congregation?

2. What are some possible dangers of NOT identifying spiritual midwives and pharaohs?

3. How might ministry be impacted if people were adept at spotting midwives and pharaohs?

4. What do you think is the best course of action when dealing with pharaohs in churches and ministries?

4

Somebody's Pregnant

The Beginning of Spiritual Births

> *"Giving birth should be your greatest*
> *achievement not your greatest fear."*
>
> **JANE WEIDEMAN**

SPIRITUAL MIDWIVES AS ENCOURAGERS

Assisting in a birth often times includes words of encouragement at the direction of the Lord. I am reminded of a vision the Lord gave me some time ago while talking to one of the spiritual mothers of my church. She had called me requesting prayer about some issues she was facing at our church. As I began to pray with her, the Lord showed me a deck of cards that had fallen on my dining room floor. Some of the cards were face up and some were face down. I began to share with her what the Lord was showing me. The description and understanding were given to me as I spoke to her. This was the message: *In order to put things in order, the Lord must have them exposed, so we will know the current order of things. It will be necessary for God to expose the disorder because we can be in such disorder for so long, that the disorder appears to be the order. Therefore, exposure of the disorder must be done so we won't reject the proper order, believing the disorder is correct.*

After I prayed for and encouraged the church mother, I began to further pray for the congregation as a whole based on what the Lord placed in my spirit. Reflecting on this event, I am now certain that during that time period, I was operating as a spiritual midwife in the role of encourager for my church family. Some of the things I was led to pray for were family relationships and marriages, the breaking of strongholds specific to the members of our church, and the issue of pride within our congregation. My prayer for the church mother eased the angst she had been feeling up until the time she had asked me to pray for her. She admitted to having felt deeply troubled in her spirit about the issues of our church. Being able to pray for her and share with her what God had shared with me, gave her hope regarding the issues of her concern.

The role of an encourager can also be spotted in our business ventures for Christ. Kristan Marshall of Absolute Tutoring Company, a business she shares with her husband, Adrian, considers herself a spiritual midwife in her work with children and youth. "A little bit of encouragement goes a long way. If I can support and develop confidence, it makes it a lot easier to elevate the student's understanding of math and science concepts."[1] God can use our talents and skills wherever we may be because we take with us what He has already put in us!

We can also observe the role of encourager in our secular professions. Orlando Arnold, professional sports agent, and owner of Pyramid Sports Group, says the principle in God's Word he uses to assist him in his effort to bring forth talent and accomplish his goals with his clients is, "That He will never forsake us, even athletes are going through battles or tough times, God is right there with them the whole time."[2] The midwife factor operates in our secular world as we encourage and support our colleagues and/or clients to achieve the goals and plans that God has established for them.

Quentin Goins, a high school band teacher, serves in the role of an encourager in his interaction with youth. Goins states, "They all have value. The goal is to help them all grow and become a better them. In my field sometimes you get a few moments, hours, a few days, a few years, and every now and then there are those that will be around for a lifetime. Growth never stops. And believe it or not, in helping them, they sometimes help the mentor and not even realize it."[3] As I said, we take God with us wherever we go. The impact we have is lasting.

If you have been called to be a spiritual midwife, you may find yourself operating in the role of encourager also. You may not have all the facts, or you may not even have a good grasp on what is occurring around you. However, God can still use you to assist others that need a welcome word of encouragement as they operate in their God-directed purpose and journey along the path God has placed them.

This reminds me of another instance where the Lord used me to be an encourager at a time when I had absolutely no clue of the inner workings of the situation the person I was called to encourage was dealing with. This time, the person I was called to encourage was Bishop Coleman (name changed for privacy), a local bishop in the Detroit metro area. The Lord prompted me to write Bishop Coleman a letter. In the letter, I simply shared what the Lord had placed on my heart. The only thing I was privy to about Bishop Coleman's situation was that the Lord had impregnated him with something and there were saboteurs waiting to control what was being birthed, since they had been unsuccessful in their attempts to destroy the "spiritual baby." Below, I have included excerpts from the letter:

> The enemy has been trying to get you to believe you are not strong enough, you are not mentally stable enough, or emotionally secure enough to handle what God has impregnated you with. GOD SAYS HE KNOWS THE PLANS HE HAS FOR YOU, PLANS TO GIVE YOU A FUTURE AND A HOPE.

> It is now that the enemy is trying to get you to abort this baby yourself, because he does not have the power, nor does he have the authority to take your lives. The attempt is to get your body, your mind, your emotions to wear out— to get weary so you would believe the LIE that you are not able to continue to carry the baby. Or worse, you will not be able to handle it after delivery.

There has been a set-up of situations to give the appearance that you can't manage physically, emotionally, or mentally. The great attempt is to get you to abort or yield control to someone else. To sign over your "parental rights" so you would have no access or authority in that which God has decided to birth through you. He has set in you something that "eye has not seen nor ear have heard." It cannot be birthed in the "old wine skins." It cannot be placed in the atmosphere of the old comfort relationships.

This NEW THING I have done requires the new covenant relationships I have set in place in order for it to develop and live and be all I have purposed it to be and do in the earth. You must "walk by faith not by sight." Do Not Embrace The Evil Report. Think of those things that are of Me.

"YOU MUST CHOOSE TO BELIEVE MY REPORT!"

—His Birthing Assistant

You're probably thinking what I was thinking when I wrote the letter—Whoa! Heavy stuff, right? You bet. But does the 'heaviness' of what God calls us to do give us a reason to shrink back? It shouldn't. God has equipped us to do the tasks He's called us to do.

When I finally ran into Bishop Coleman after sending him this unsolicited letter from God, he shared with me that he had been dealing with personal matters that had left him feeling defeated and emotionally drained. He didn't tell me what those matters were, but it was apparent that what God had shared with me was somewhat of a lifesaver for Bishop Coleman. This is a prime example of why the office of the spiritual midwife needs to be taken seriously. More importantly, those who are called to the positions of spiritual midwives, MUST be obedient to the move of God. Others are depending on our obedience!

THE MIDWIFE FACTOR MEDITATION

- *Assisting in a spiritual birth may involve giving words of encouragement from the Lord. One of the ways to spot spiritual midwives is their fear of God.*

- *Those who are called to the positions of spiritual midwives, MUST be obedient to the move of God even when we feel personally uncomfortable with an assignment. Others are depending on our obedience!*

- *As a spiritual midwife, God can use you as an encourager even when you don't know all the facts.*

THE MIDWIFE FACTOR
ESSENTIAL CARE REFLECTION

1. Reflecting on both situations presented in this chapter, how do you think you would have handled each as a spiritual midwife? Why?

2. What do you think could cause someone who is called as a spiritual midwife to hesitate to act when given a word/ directive from God?

3. In Chapter 1, I discussed how I often found myself in situations and meetings I hadn't planned to be in. In this chapter I've shared visions the Lord has given me concerning encouraging others. Tell about how you or someone you know have had similar experiences and how those experiences were handled, especially if someone questioned the "right" of the spiritual midwife to be involved.

4. What exactly do you believe obedience looks like when faced with unfamiliar or uncomfortable circumstances? Talk about ways spiritual midwives can navigate these challenges.

5

Complications

Resistance to New Ministries and New Ideas

"You are not to focus on the difficulties, pain, or discomfort of an assignment, but that your focus is to be on the "able ness" of God."

BISHOP NED ADAMS

STUCK

There are books, ideas, dreams, businesses, and ministries that are stuck in the birth canal. Stuck in the birthing canal because of fear of the birth: the changes it will bring, the people it will involve or exclude. The bigness of it overwhelms you—the thought of "Who am I to do this"? As Bishop Adams states, your focus is to be on the "able ness" of God. For example, are you among those that know the title of the book you are to write *someday*? Do you have a book in your belly, a title jotted down on some notepad or journal, or just something in your mind, waiting for *someday*? You may even understand how greatly the information you possess can benefit the Kingdom, but it is still positioned in the birth canal, ready for the *delivery*.

Courage is needed to move forward with an idea or dream—especially when we don't think we are good enough or when we compare our dreams with those of others. There are people waiting for what's in your belly—your birth canal. Do not be among those that went to the grave with the babies still in their wombs. You may be someone's midwife factor in their deliverance, repentance, conversion, or ministry for the Kingdom's sake. "Today, when you hear his voice don't harden your hearts …" (Hebrews 3:15). Don't stop the contractions, advance toward the delivery. Push to assist in birthing what God has seen fit to bring forth through you. "For I am not ashamed of this Good News about Christ. It is the power of God at work, saving everyone who believes—the Jew first and also the Gentile" (Romans 1:16).

EMERGENCY DELIVERY

Some births require an emergency delivery because the birth canal is void of water. When it became time for the birth of my first child, my body began to align and position for her to be delivered. With the start of the contractions, my water sac broke, leaving my baby void of the protective water that had been surrounding her. Soon the uterus stopped all contractions. There was no movement to bring her forth. Everything that needed to happen to bring forth the birth had stopped.

Because my water sack had already broken, my doctor told me that I was in a dangerous position and susceptible to an infection. He needed to induce labor to help the uterus do its work. The doctor informed me that my uterus had become "lazy" and he would need to inject medication into my IV that would cause the uterus to contract and do its work. Some of us need an injection in our IV lines—the midwife factor, a spiritual midwife to stimulate and assist the advancement of our deliveries that are needed for the work of ministry and the advancement of the Kingdom.

The water has broken, and the births are being threatened and are subject to infection, contamination, or injury. Water is necessary for life. Jesus told the woman at the well, that He was the Living Water (John 4:10-13). Because of Christ, she would never thirst again. The Prophet Jeremiah describes God as the spring of living water (Jeremiah 2:13). Some reasons for the womb being void of water is because of unbelief, turning away, forsaking what the Lord has called you to do or to be (Jeremiah 17:13). If you are thirsty, seem to be lacking the benefits of living water, feeling the effects of a dry spell, falling into unbelief, experiencing contamination, seek the living water that satisfies the deepest need. Its supply is inexhaustible, it is not affected by time or seasons, it makes life fruitful, it is available for all to partake (see John 4:10, 14; 7:37-38; Zechariah 14:8; Revelation 7:17; 22:1,2, 17). Jesus says, "Anyone who believes in me may come and drink! For the Scriptures declare, 'Rivers of living water will flow from his heart.'" (John 7:38)

THE COMPLICATIONS
OF CRITICISM AND DOUBT

"You're not a leader. Why did you even accept this position? You don't have any leadership skills." Those were the wounding words that were hurled at me after I had been promoted to chair for a ministry and had led a week-long ministry event. No, they didn't come from an enemy or a disgruntled event attendee. They came from two so-called friends who ambushed me (they really just pulled me aside—don't get too worried) right after the event. Talk about church hurts!

What made this situation even more bizarre and painful was that I had been *recommended* for the position by a few church leaders and approved by my then pastor. I'm certain these experienced ministry leaders felt that I was qualified for the position, or they never would have given me a thumbs up. And you know what? The event was successful. Yes, there were a few hiccups, like anyone would experience while planning a week-long event. Nonetheless, it was a success!

So why did my two "friends" (and I certainly hope you don't have any friends like these) say all these negative and hurtful things to me—even going so far as to criticize the outfit I wore? Simply because they didn't *see* what God was doing with me, in me, and through me! They were attempting to impose *their* thoughts of who and what I *should be* on me. Unbeknownst to them, they were acting as pharaohs—attempting to discourage me from pursuing the work God had called me to do. These loaded, hurtful statements had the potential to be confidence killers—spiritual midwife complications of criticism and doubts. But I prevailed. And you will too.

You must be careful not to reject what God has deposited within you, based on others' taste or what they believe is best for you. My two so-called friends didn't view me as a leader; they didn't see me as a person who possessed leadership skills. They questioned my abilities; more importantly, they were questioning God Himself. Because if you believe all those leaders—including my then-pastor—gave the green light for me to head that event without them seeking God in prayer, I've got some land I want to sell you in the Everglades (wink).

Often criticizers and doubters are content with you just surviving— not growing and multiplying. Their main problem may be that the "new wine" (what you are carrying and developing for the Kingdom's sake) you present is too rich for their systems and they believe it must be too rich for yours too! Their objection or need to discourage you may stem from the belief that you are inadequate just because God has not found them to be F.A.T. (faithful, available, and teachable) Christians. They have convinced themselves that you are not capable of handling tasks, dreams, ministries, or inventions because they are not willing to experience change. It has nothing to do with your capabilities.

Therefore, God in His wisdom, knows not to pour out the new wine for them because it would destroy, harm, or make them ill because their systems are unable to handle the total life stewardship that is necessary concerning the responsibilities, blessings, challenges, and advancement that comes with the possession, consumption, and distribution of the new wine. When new wine is given, it is because you need it, and it is good for the Kingdom's sake. A spiritual midwife gains a deeper level of understanding when he or she can discern new wine when someone is pregnant and is in need of the midwife factor.

DOUBLE-O-SILENCE

I'm sure you've heard of 007, the fictitious James Bond spy-character, who was skilled at keeping all manner of secrets. Well, hold on to your church hat! Be aware that not everything that God gives you should be shared immediately—not even with those who are closest to you in your inner circle. Sometimes, you've got to take a page right out of 007's play book and keep some secrets and remain silent. Because of human beings' natural resistance to change, be careful as you begin to share your God given dreams. Pray that God will give you His wisdom and discernment to be able to identify those around you who will support you and do not have an agenda to impede your progress or interfere with you moving beyond your comfort zone and embracing the change opportunities that are sent your way by God.

When it comes to dreams and visions, we've got to remember our good ole brother Joseph way back in Genesis. His near-fatal mistake was revealing to his brothers the dream that God had given him:

> One night Joseph had a dream, and when he told his brothers about it, they hated him more than ever. "Listen to this dream," he said. "We were out in the field, tying up bundles of grain. Suddenly my bundle stood up, and your bundles all gathered around and bowed low before mine!" His brothers responded, "So you think you will be our king, do you? Do you actually think you will reign over us?" And they hated him all the more because of his dreams and the way he talked about them. Soon Joseph had another dream, and again he told his brothers about it. "Listen, I have had another dream," he said. "The sun, moon, and eleven stars bowed low before me!" This time he told the dream to his father as well as to his brothers, but his father scolded him. "What kind of dream is that?" he asked. "Will your mother and I and your brothers actually come and bow to the ground before you?" (Genesis 37:5-10).

Do you remember what happened next? Joseph's brothers' hate grew into a plan to kill him, but then finally morphed into a plan to sell him into slavery instead. They weren't trying to hear Joseph's dream of greatness—especially over them. The takeaway in this lesson is that everyone will not be able to accept the dreams and visions God gives you. Instead of being supportive, they may go out of their way to sabotage (I hope not as far as Joseph's brothers) or belittle you and cause you to sabotage your dreams with self-doubt.

There will be those who will not always understand why you even want to consider trying something new especially if it appears that your present situation is at survival level. It is the "Why rock the boat?" mentality. Caution is also needed in placing your new wine in the old wineskins of unstable and uncharted relationships. There are those who have become attachments to you, your ministry, and your family because of what you are carrying. Like Simon in Acts 8:9-24, who offered to pay the Apostles for the power they had because he wanted to do the miracles that he saw them do. Some will not realize that the power in you comes from the Holy Spirit. They may want to be a part of what you are doing, although God has not called them to it. Your guard at this stage of the pregnancy must be on alert 24/7.

THE COMPLICATION OF INVITATION

Do you remember as a kid when you were told by your parents to do something—not your brothers or sisters, not the neighbor next door—just you, and because you felt like a little assistance would be a great idea to help you get the task done more quickly, you enlisted the help of someone else? Perhaps you even passed the task off to a younger sibling. Let me tell you, that may have been an ingenious idea that help to hone the managerial skills you have today, but God's Kingdom doesn't work that way. When God gives you an assignment, He's giving it to you. Unless you have a release from God to involve others in the plan, I would strongly recommend that you don't. In some cases, inviting others to join you on an assignment you've been given by God may result in an unwanted outcome.

God will teach your hands to war (see Psalms 18:34, 144:1). God's plan can't be altered. You must not allow people or circumstances to cause you to be diverted or distracted from what He has called you to do or to be. Be very careful inviting or allowing others to join in the work God has anointed you to do. You may be hindering a blessing

God has prepared for you. Your hands have been strengthened for a specific work, if others do what God has given you to do it will have a different effect and different results because of the experiences and associations they have been exposed to during their lives. The vision or plan will not be fulfilled or carried out to its fullest without all the factors you bring to the birthing.

THE COMPLICATION OF SELF-SABOTAGE

I've talked about how others can complicate and sabotage spiritual births, but what happens when the saboteur is you??? Hmm… Now that is a great question! How could you, a spiritual midwife, who is called by God to do a task, sabotage your mission? Remember what I said about how my two so-called friends ambushed me with their negativity? What if I had allowed their words to seep in my spirit, and I began to believe what they said about me? What if I questioned my ability to lead? What if I just accepted their report that I didn't have any leadership skills? What do you think would have happened the next time I received an assignment? If you guessed that I would probably be reluctant or lack confidence the next time, you get a prize!

We can sabotage ourselves with a lack of confidence because a lack of confidence causes us to hesitate when God calls us to do something. To be clear, the foundation of our confidence does not lie in our skills, achievements, etc.… But instead, it lies in what some call "Godfidence," the belief that God has given us what we need. We can be confident that we can do all He calls us to do because of His strength—not our own.

Hesitation is out of alignment with God's will. Like the "friends" who questioned what God had called me to do, when you hesitate, you are questioning God's wisdom. After all, He knows what He put in you. If He gives you a task, you better believe He has equipped you for it. In Exodus 3:10-11 when the Lord called Moses to go to Pharaoh and bring the children of Israel out of bondage, Moses seemed to be plagued with self-doubt. In fact, he is a perfect example of questioning God's wisdom and attempting self-sabotage:

> "Come now, therefore, and I will send thee unto Pharaoh,
> that thou mayest bring forth my people the children of
> Israel out of Egypt. And Moses said unto God, Who am
> I that I should go unto Pharaoh, and that I should bring
> the children of Israel out of Egypt?" (Exodus 3:10-11, *KJV*)

Do you see how God *told* Moses the plan, but Moses *questioned* God's plan? The plan was simple and specific. God spoke two key phrases to Moses in this passage. The first is: "I will send..." The next is: "That you may bring..." How specific can you get? God was going to do something. Then Moses was going to do something. If you pay close attention, you will realize that God said He would do His part of the plan FIRST. But boy oh boy, notice what Moses asked God: "Who am I that I should go to Pharaoh, and that I should bring the children of Israel out of Egypt?" Wow. Now listen, I don't want to beat up on Moses too badly because we all suffer from self-doubt from time to time, but God clearly knew how the plan was supposed to go down. Moses was pushing back with the question that many of us struggle with from time to time: "Who am I that I should _____?" You can fill in the blank with almost anything you want. In the end, this is nothing but plain old self-doubt. And if that wasn't bad enough, further in Exodus 4:10-14, Moses attempts to engage in self-sabotage:

> But Moses pleaded with the Lord, "O Lord, I'm not very
> good with words. I never have been, and I'm not now, even
> though you have spoken to me. I get tongue-tied, and my
> words get tangled." Then the Lord asked Moses, "Who
> makes a person's mouth? Who decides whether people
> speak or do not speak, hear or do not hear, see or do not
> see? Is it not I, the Lord? Now go! I will be with you as you
> speak, and I will instruct you in what to say." But Moses
> again pleaded, "Lord, please! Send anyone else." Then the
> Lord became angry with Moses. "All right," he said. "What
> about your brother, Aaron the Levite? I know he speaks
> well. And look! He is on his way to meet you now. He will
> be delighted to see you (Exodus 4:10-14).

In the preceding passage, Moses calls himself informing (eye roll) God why His plan isn't a good one. This time, Moses focuses on his apparent speech problem. And God fires a few rhetorical questions back at Moses to remind him that it is God who made mouths in the first place, and God who decides whether people speak or not. The Lord even assures Moses that He will go with him. What better help does Moses need? God will go with him! But that wasn't good enough either, so Moses finally tells God, (and I'm paraphrasing) "Hey, just please send someone else—anyone else but me." And Scripture reveals that made God angry. What a terrible predicament to be in, having God angry with you because you are shunning the perfect plan He has for you!

God knows your strengths and capabilities. He knows your weaknesses and your failures. Before He assigns you to a task, He has taken all these things into consideration. Because He is a good, faithful, and loving God, He assigns us tasks anyway—despite our many flaws. It is a privilege to work with God in ministry. He doesn't have to use us. He chooses to use us—with all our baggage and push back, God uses us to help others for His glory.

You have been prepared for such a time as this with your unique signature. Your discernment will mature through your trust in, obedience, and commitment to the Lord. This gift is needed when warring for what God has said about you, others, or a situation. You will experience the birthing in its fullness of growth, influence, productivity, and favor as you rely on, trust in, and advance toward the Lord.

Pray that the Lord fulfills His purposes and ask Him to resurrect the lifeless spiritual babies in the wombs of His people and grant them wisdom to induce the contractions to be fruitful and multiply. Your ideas are needed in the Kingdom now. It's time to seek out a spiritual midwife that can assist you through intercession, encouragement, warning, equipping, teaching, demonstrating, and listening as you live your faith out loud through our Lord and Savior, Jesus Christ.

THE MIDWIFE FACTOR MEDITATION

- *God desires F.A.T. (Faithful. Available. Teachable.) Christians.*

- *Before sharing your dreams or visions with anyone, pray that God will give you His wisdom and discernment to be able to identify those around you who will support you and not have an agenda to impede your progress.*

- *You must not allow people or circumstances to cause you to be diverted or distracted from what God has called you to do or to be.*

- *In order not to hinder your blessings, be very careful inviting or allowing others to join in the work God has anointed you to do.*

- *You must not allow your personal weaknesses or insecurities to keep you from obeying what God calls you to do.*

THE MIDWIFE FACTOR
ESSENTIAL CARE REFLECTION

1. When all the books and dreams that are stuck inside of people are finally ready to be birthed, where do you think the publishers, editors, and graphic artists will be found?

2. Is there a need for someone to induce the contractions to bring you from the state of stuck to bring forth your deliverance? Do you need a spiritual midwife because of what is in your birth canal?

3. What spiritual midwife duties are you currently engaged in?

4. What self-criticisms, self-doubt, or self-sabotage have you experienced/engaged in? Is this an ongoing problem for you? Have you resolved these issues? If not, how do you deal with these issues?

5. Tell about a situation or experience where you were faced with people criticizing or questioning your abilities. How did you handle it?

6

Pregnancy Risks

The Dangers of Serving as a Spiritual Midwife

> *"Mentoring moments may not be prolonged, but when someone whom you respect says just the right words or gives you the attention when you need it the most, that affect can last a lifetime."*
>
> **BETTY SOUTHHARD**

THE RISK OF BEING BARREN

What if you've prepared to be a spiritual midwife, but you don't feel like the Lord has given you an assignment? And what do you do when it looks like others have found their calling in various ministries, but you're unsure about how you should be assisting? You may be beginning to feel barren. Barrenness is a definite risk to spiritual new births.

Merriam Webster's Dictionary describes barrenness as *not producing, not productive, and devoid and lacking.*[1] For the spiritual midwife, a state of barrenness can range from one being unproductive after unsuccessful attempts to be productive, to one who is being unproductive because he or she chose to take no action. Barrenness can also mean

65

experiencing fruitless results, subsequently causing feelings of useless-ness. Mentally, prolonged feelings of uselessness can lead to a spiritual midwife feeling lonely, empty, and depleted. This can open the door to the spirit of desolation and depression.

ARE YOU REALLY BARREN?

I believe the state of barrenness can occur as a result of unbelief, fear, lack of faith, unforgiveness, pride, and/or disobedience. How do we rectify our situation and become fruitful again when this is the case? I think we need to start with self-examination as it says in Lamentations 3:40, "Instead, let us test and examine our ways. Let us turn back to the Lord."

When our barrenness problem stems from within, we need to do a Midwife Factor Spiritual Self-Check.

THE MIDWIFE FACTOR SPIRITUAL SELF-CHECK
1. Is there some sin in my life that needs to be eradicated?
2. Have I delayed in doing something the Lord asked me to do?
3. Have I been negligent in completing the small tasks I've been assigned?
4. Do I exhibit a servant's attitude as I work with others?
5. Do I keep my pride in check, remembering that my gifts are from God?
6. Have I demonstrated unforgiveness toward anyone?
7. Do I have a spirit of resentment?
8. Do I demonstrate unchecked anger?
9. Have I operated with a lack of faith?
10. Do I demonstrate the fruit of the Spirit?

When we assess/examine ourselves, we leave room to make necessary behavioral and spiritual changes. We make room to repent and ask

God for forgiveness. If you are dealing with unbelief or a lack of faith pray and ask God to help your unbelief. If you have unforgiveness in your heart towards someone else, yourself, or even God, pray and ask Him to help you forgive. If pride has entered in your heart, pray, and ask God to move it. Reflect on your behavior and correct your thinking so that you can be positioned to receive as you converse with the Lord, worship Him, and grow your faith in the One who is faithful. We must pray and ask God to examine us and show us how to please Him as David did.

> Search me, O God, and know my heart;
> test me and know my anxious thoughts.
> Point out anything in me that offends you,
> and lead me along the path of everlasting life
> (Psalm 139:23-24).

FALSE BARRENNESS

A false sense of barrenness can be caused by what I call a "spiritual smokescreen"—something that temporarily hides conception. A spiritual smokescreen can appear due to life events and other distractions that steal your focus/attention away from what God is instructing you to do as a spiritual midwife. When this occurs, without consulting the Lord in prayer, you may have thoughts and beliefs that you are barren.

This false sense of barrenness can trick you into thinking that you are unable to conceive (help bring forth a new ministry or project) or trick you into believing you will miscarry (not be able to complete a ministry or project). You may feel undeserving of being blessed by God, question God, or succumb to feelings of unworthiness like Moses. Ask God to help you with these emotions so that He can work through you.

Barrenness is not always a permanent condition as is reported in God's Word in Hebrews 11:11, *HCSB*, "By faith Sarah herself also received strength to conceive seed, and she bore a child when she was past the age, because she judged Him faithful who had promised." We also find that after conversations with the Lord, concerning her barrenness, Hannah's prayers and worship resulted in God opening her womb and she conceived (1 Samuel Chapter 1). The spiritual season of barrenness is not a doomsday report because God wastes nothing. He is always up to something.

USED IN YOUR BARREN SEASON

One of the most devastating and challenging periods of my life was when I was going through a divorce. During that season in my life, I felt less effective. Stripped. Shamed. "Who am I to minister to anyone now? How can God use me?" These were the questions I asked God and myself. Like The Scarlet Letter, I felt like I had a big *Divorce* sign written on me. Strangely enough, however, it was during this time that married people in my life begin to reach out to me for counsel on their marital problems. It was unreal. All I could think about was, "Why are they coming to me?"

One day when I received a call from a close friend venting about her marriage and seeking counsel, I had to stop her mid-way through her spiel and say, "Uh…you do realize I'm going through a divorce right now, don't you???" But folk continued to call me, stop by, tell me about their marital problems, and seek my advice. And I'm happy to report that the three main people who sought me out during what I thought was my barren season, are still happily married—for over thirty years. One remained married until her husband passed just a few years ago.

Even in my brokenness and heartbreak, God used me to impart wisdom to those who needed it most. He used me to help save the marriages of others even though my situation seemed barren. I couldn't change my circumstances, but I could share the knowledge I had gained through my painful experience, and I could share God's Word with those who were seeking help. God desires to use us even when we feel unusable. Our barrenness may be God's cultivation location.

The ministry of helps-deliverance ministers to us during our hurts and circumstances. God has required us to minister to others experiencing similar, if not the same hurts and circumstances. 2 Corinthians 1:3-4, *NIV*, says, "Praise be to the God and Father of our Lord Jesus Christ, the Father of compassion and the God of all comfort, who comforts us in all our troubles, so that we can comfort those in any trouble with the comfort we ourselves receive from God."

This demonstrates God's love and how His healing and wholeness can be accomplished. The account in John 6:1-15 of the multiplication of the loaves of bread and fish, demonstrate an opportunity for God to multiply your present provisions and then use you as an instrument to bless, feed, and nourish others while representing Him. You are empowered to use the residuals of what has been ministered to you and share it with others. It is through our availability that He has made available to us a more intimate relationship with Him as we assist others. Our transparency in sharing our testimonies with others gives us the privilege of comforting them. Risking the exposure of our emotional and spiritual vulnerability to let someone know he or she is not alone is worth the risk and provides an opportunity for our faith and their faith to increase.

Your situation may be that God has selected you, anointed you, and given you the capacity to mother someone else's child or children (i.e., assist another spiritual midwife with a new birth). Just like in the natural realm when a woman with no children of her own shows love to children who did not come from her womb, you may be called in this season to encourage and to help another spiritual midwife to birth, love, support, and nurture something that God is bringing forth.

God is no stranger to "spiritual adoptions." He used Pharaoh's daughter to adopt Moses so He could do great things in Moses' life and in the lives of the Children of Israel (see Exodus 2). He will use you for His good pleasure. As it states in Philippians 2:13, "For God is working in you, giving you the desire and the power to do what pleases Him." If you do find yourself in a barren season, be open to the move of God.

RISKS WORTH TAKING

Risks come with the territory of serving as a spiritual midwife. Be aware that your role may make you susceptible to rejection, loneliness, and detachment. This role in the ministry of helps is often a behind the scenes operation. I want to caution you that no matter how much you invest in the one giving the birth or the birthing process itself, you must not become possessive. Yes, you may put your blood, sweat and tears into getting a ministry or project off the ground only to have to leave it in the hands of someone else, but don't ever forget that you are on assignment. It's not about you. It's about the work of the Kingdom.

You must discern when God is directing you and giving you the power to walk away from the things you help birth. It will seem at times that the credit, acknowledgement, and accolades for the work you have done in implementing creative ideas, plans, and proposals, will be given to others. Remember it is God who worked through you to accomplish these tasks. You must remain focused on the fact that your work in this ministry is for the Glory of God; it is indeed worth the risk of being overlooked.

Like with the natural midwife, it does not matter how difficult the process becomes for you to help deliver the birth, or how much time, energy, and ideas you invest; it is still the child of the one who was impregnated. It's the same with spiritual pregnancies. At times, even after the birth, the pregnant one is sometimes so weakened that a spiritual midwife may find that they must care for both the one who gave birth and that which was birthed. You may have to step in and lead the project, ministry, or group for a short period of time, with the understanding that you will relinquish your leadership when the called one is ready to take over.

THE MIDWIFE FACTOR MEDITATION

- *A state of barrenness can occur as a result of unbelief, fear, lack of faith, unforgiveness, pride, and/or disobedience.*

- *Spiritual midwives must conduct spiritual self-checks in order to examine their lives and behavior that may cause them to be in a barren season.*

- *God can still use you to bless others during your barren season.*

- *Remembering that you are on an assignment from God can prevent you from getting possessive about the ministries you assist and help you to willingly release leadership when it's necessary to move on.*

THE MIDWIFE FACTOR
ESSENTIAL CARE REFLECTION

1. How do you conduct spiritual self-examinations?

2. How has God used you to minister to others during a seemingly barren season?

3. How does it affect you for others to receive recognition or accolades for the work you have done as a spiritual midwife?

4. Conduct the Midwife Factor Self-Check. Which questions did you respond with a "yes"?

7

Delivery

Transformation and Results

*"Live a transformed life so others might see the light
and be affected by the salt that is produced."*

AUDREY MCGRESHAM

What comes to mind when you think of the word *transforma-tion*? Do you think of a sudden change or a gradual process of *becoming*? A church member and friend of mine shared her experience about the day she was baptized some years ago. She said she remembered being lifted out of the water by a minister who exclaimed, "Walk in the newness of life!" and although she was excited and overcome with emotion about her new relationship with Christ, my friend said she didn't quite feel "new."

She knew of course that she was saved because she had confessed that Jesus is Lord, believed He died for her sins, and that God had raised Him from the dead. She understood that her baptism had been an outward symbol of her confession. However, her expectations of being "new" didn't match what she felt. In fact, she said she felt like the same person! What she discovered in her walk with Christ, being under good teaching and studying the Word for herself was: although she felt like the same person, a spiritual renewal had taken place in her by way of the Holy Spirit. She had been born again. The *Holman*

Christian Standard Bible tells us in Titus 3:5, "He saved us—not by works of righteousness that we had done, but according to His mercy, through the washing of regeneration and renewal by the Holy Spirit." This is the starting point of our transformation in Christ as our transformation is an ongoing spiritual process by which we allow the Holy Spirit to work in us as we renew our mind, thoughts, and actions to align with what Christ says.

TRANSFORMATION

What does transformation look like? If it's an inward process, how do we know it's occurring? Unlike my friend, as a new Christian we shouldn't base our transformation on how we feel but rather our submission to Christ. There can be no results in ministry without transformed people! In Romans 12:2, Paul reminds us, "Don't copy the behavior and customs of this world, but let God transform you into a new person by changing the way you think. Then you will learn to know God's will for you, which is good and pleasing and perfect." So, to answer the question, "What does transformation look like?" it looks like a person who is allowing God to make them into the person He wants them to be. Our part in our transformation is to *submit* ourselves by changing the way we think because changing the way we think influences our attitudes, beliefs, and how we ultimately live our lives.

When we change how we think and begin to agree with God, we become what He intends for us to be—more like Him. Have you ever been told as a child or an adult that you look like one or both of your parents? No matter how old you are, this always seems to make parents smile and beam with pride. Well, you know what? I imagine that our Divine Father smiles and beams with satisfaction when we look like Jesus in our thoughts and actions—when we let the Word of God govern our lives instead of the outside influences of the world. In 2 Corinthians 3:17-18 Paul states, "For the Lord is the Spirit, and wherever the Spirit of the Lord is, there is freedom. So all of us who have had that veil removed can see and reflect the glory of the Lord. And the Lord—who is the Spirit—makes us more and more like Him as we are changed into His glorious image." The purpose of ongoing transformation in the life of the believer is to become like Jesus.

RENEWED MINDS

Transformation occurs by the renewing of our minds. This is us aligning our thoughts and beliefs with God's. Scripture teaches us how to do our part in this process:

> And so, dear brothers and sisters, I plead with you to give your bodies to God because of all he has done for you. Let them be a living and holy sacrifice—the kind he will find acceptable. This is truly the way to worship him. Don't copy the behavior and customs of this world, but let God transform you into a new person by changing the way you think. Then you will learn to know God's will for you, which is good and pleasing and perfect (Romans 12:1-2).

Here we see that we are expected to give God all of us. Our bodies become living sacrifices to God—meaning we are His to use for His will—not the things of the world. We're admonished not to copy the behavior and customs of this world. The only way to be successful at that when we live in a culture that clamors to conform us to its ways and seeks our attention at every angle, is to change how we view things. We change the way we think, and God transforms us. This is how we please God.

I don't know if you've ever had to purchase a gift for someone you didn't know that well. For me, it's extremely difficult. I know what I like, but that doesn't mean the person I'm buying for is going to be happy with the gift I like. It's hard to please someone when you have no idea how to please them. How can we please God if we don't know what is pleasing to Him? We must learn to please God by reading His Word—it's His love letter to us. His revelation of Himself. We must educate ourselves on the ways of God.

Christian education is needed for our personal transformation as well as the transformations of those we disciple. Our goal in sharing the Gospel message and teaching the Word of God is so that lives are transformed—not just any old transformation, but one that accomplishes God's purpose in our lives. Gary Newton described the importance of transformational teaching in his book, *Heart-Deep Teaching: Engaging Students for Transformed Lives*:

> The goal of Christian education must be to transform the heart so that every aspect of the person becomes progressively more Christlike. Anything less denies the radical transformational power that Christ gave us through His grace and Holy Spirit. Learning must penetrate the surface of the mind, the emotions, the will, and behavior. Heart-deep teaching must affect the innermost core of the person.[1]

I once heard a minister say about church, "You shouldn't leave out the same way you came in," meaning the message or lesson that you received should cause a Christlike change in you. Newton addressed this when he said, "learning must penetrate the surface." It's not enough to sit under good teaching or preaching. We have to allow the Word to flow deep into our beings.

TRANSFORMATION OF A SPIRITUAL MIDWIFE

As you submit to the calling of being a spiritual midwife and coach other spiritual midwives, you yourself must ensure that you are constantly renewing *your* mind to provide the best support to the persons God has entrusted to you to mentor. I'd like us to take a closer look at the commands in Romans 12:2 and focus on practically engaging in four key areas:

1. Present your body as a living and holy sacrifice.

2. Don't copy the behavior of the world.

3. Renew your mind.

4. Find out what is pleasing to God.

We have been taught to consider ourselves as the bosses of our bodies, our time, our possessions, etc.... But this is contrary to presenting ourselves as a sacrifice. Sacrificing means to give up something. We are giving our very selves to God. Our bodies are His to do as He wishes for His glory. This includes being like Jesus and helping others. The poem, Christ Has No Body by St. Teresa of Avila sums it up perfectly:

"Christ Has No Body"

Christ has no body but yours,
No hands, no feet on earth but yours,
Yours are the eyes with which he looks
Compassion on this world,
Yours are the feet with which he walks to do good,
Yours are the hands, with which he blesses all the world.
Yours are the hands, yours are the feet,
Yours are the eyes, you are his body.
Christ has no body now but yours,
No hands, no feet on earth but yours,
Yours are the eyes with which he looks
compassion on this world.
Christ has no body now on earth but yours.[2]

How much more eloquently can it be stated? We are the hands and feet of Christ on this earth. This is our sacrifice.

Businesses sometimes use more wisdom than churches when it comes to succession planning – the strategy of identifying and developing future leaders in an organization in order to pass the mantle. Our true guide to ministry doesn't lie in business models of the world. The Bible has it all laid out! Was not Paul doing succession planning as he mentored Timothy? Did he not provide instruction and direction so that Timothy would be prepared to carry out the mission of Christ even when Paul was no longer with him? And Jesus was the greatest succession planner of them all as He continually prepared His disciples for His departure: teaching them how to pray, how to teach, how to baptize and make disciples of all men.

My point is: there is no reason for us to look to the world to be our guide or model for anything—business related or otherwise. The answers we need are in the Bible. We can keep ourselves from influence of the culture by comparing everything with the Word of God. The litmus test of any situation or influence is to see if it aligns with God's Word. If it doesn't align, it must go! We cannot be consumed with fitting into the culture. As we train other spiritual midwives, we must constantly live radically in that we remain culture-opposed and God-obsessed! Our mentees will be looking to us as models. Our lives should reflect that we are followers of God—not the world. This should be evident in our speech, our response to situations, our faith, and our practice of spiritual disciplines: such as worship, prayer, study, and meditation. Not copying the behaviors of the world is simply copying the behaviors of Christ!

If we copy the behaviors of Christ, the renewing of our minds will occur simultaneously. We are to actively engage our transformation process. Remember we do the renewing as God does the transforming. We are partners with God in our transformation. The Greek word for renew is *anakainoo,* which means to renovate. Imagine that. I'm sure you've seen those television shows where professional contractors go in and totally gut a home, transforming it into a gorgeous new abode that looks absolutely nothing like the original. I love a good home makeover show! In most of the properties, contractors take the walls all the way down to the studs and get rid of everything in the house that is of no use.

Every so often in these kinds of properties, there may be an antique clawfoot tub or a turn-of-the-century brick fireplace that is salvaged and restored to its natural luster. Now imagine your mind as the house that is in need of a spiritual "gutting" every day. Take it all the way down to the studs—getting rid of any thoughts or cultural influences that don't align with God's word. Salvage all the things of God, good thoughts, spiritual practices, and restore them to their original luster. Remember when you first came into a relationship with God? You were probably as on fire for Him as I was. The renewing of the mind includes loving the Word and seeking God as eagerly as we did in the beginning of our relationship with Him—giving our connection a new shine!

When I think of the fourth key area of Romans 12:1-2, which is demonstrating a life that is pleasing God, the first thing I think of is emulating Jesus as a servant. I picture the Lord feeding the poor, attending to the needs of widows, uplifting those who society has seemingly forgotten. I think of a life of service and upright living. I think of treating others with compassion and having patience. Knowing God in an intimate way should cause us to reflect His ways. Community is important to God. How we treat others is important to God. We can please Him by taking the knowledge we have of Him and emulating Him in our service to one another. The transformation of a spiritual midwife should include service to others. This may be serving as a coach or mentor as well as assisting in other ministries that serve less fortunate individuals or communities.

TRANSFORMATION OF THE CHURCH

You've probably heard this before but it's worth saying again: There can be no transformation of the church unless the folk who make up the church are transformed! Believers are the body of Christ—we are His church. There are no perfect churches because there are no perfect people. With that being said, we can work toward perfection by honoring what God has placed in us. When there is a transformation of the church, we will see transformation in communities. It starts with individual believers availing themselves to God mentally, spiritually, and physically. Ephesians 4: 11-16 puts it this way:

> Now these are the gifts Christ gave to the church: the apostles, the prophets, the evangelists, and the pastors and teachers. Their responsibility is to equip God's people to do his work and build up the church, the body of Christ. This will continue until we all come to such unity in our faith and knowledge of God's Son that we will be mature in the Lord, measuring up to the full and complete standard of Christ.
>
> Then we will no longer be immature like children. We won't be tossed and blown about by every wind of new

teaching. We will not be influenced when people try to trick us with lies so clever they sound like the truth. Instead, we will speak the truth in love, growing in every way more and more like Christ, who is the head of his body, the church. He makes the whole body fit together perfectly. As each part does its own special work, it helps the other parts grow, so that the whole body is healthy and growing and full of love (Ephesians 4:11-16).

What a beautiful vision of the church, everyone working in his/her gifted areas, equipping others! Here Paul emphasizes what is necessary: unity in faith and unity in the church. We must have an undiluted understanding of the Gospel message. The goal is to have maturity, truth, and love. To achieve this the church must be clear on four essential questions:

1. What does the church believe about Christ?

   Is the church clear on the knowledge of who Jesus is according to His Word so that it does not stray from the truth of the Gospel?

2. How does the church minister to its people?

   Is the church a supportive place where people can mature spiritually under sound doctrine?

3. How do the people of the church exercise their gifts?

   Are people operating in their gifts unselfishly?

4. How does the exercising of gifts affect the communities at large?

   Is the larger community that the church serves being changed for the better because of the work of the church through the message of Christ?

RESULTS

Results come when obedience abounds. Think about how much believers can change the world by applying the principles in Romans. We would see improvement in every area of our lives. Our personal transformations would extend beyond the borders of the church into our places of work and every business or community project that God assigns us.

Dr. Otis McGresham, Prevention Educator and Victim Resource Specialist for the Project Safe Center at Vanderbilt University, a resource center for those impacted by sexual and intimate partner violence states:

> To put it simply, I model the behavior that I wish to see in others. Behavior that will lead to communities where interpersonal violence can't happen because all of the community members work to prevent it from happening. And a community where we take care of anyone who has been harmed in a caring, empathetic way that responds to their unique needs. Opening people's eyes to the everyday opportunities that they have to make their community a safer place is something that I am hopeful they practice in the educational environment that I help to create, and they take with them out into the world when they graduate. I don't approach my work from a specific spiritual lens. However, there is a significant alignment between my prevention efforts and Christlike behavior. The community that I am working to create is a reflection of the world that Jesus talked about. Caring for others and creating a community where people are safe from harm is congruent with what He asks of us.[3]

Even in his secular role, Dr. McGresham demonstrates how an individual can use his/her gifts to impact the whole of society for positive change. Our secular work should always be an extension of who we are as believers in Christ. We may not legally be able to promote Christ on our jobs the way we are allowed to outside of our businesses, but our attitudes, work ethic, and heart for the people we serve should reflect Christ for ultimate results in working with and for others.

THE MIDWIFE FACTOR
AFTER-DELIVERY MEDITATION

- *Transformation is an ongoing process of the Holy Spirit that occurs in believers as we renew our minds.*

- *We must change how we think to agree with God.*

- *Our bodies should be presented as holy and living sacrifices for God's use.*

- *True spiritual transformation in believers will lead to transformed churches and transformed communities.*

- *Results occur when believers mature in their faith and use their gifts with obedience.*

THE MIDWIFE FACTOR
AFTER-DELIVERY REFLECTION

1. What is the importance of spiritual maturity?

2. What is your understanding of the truth of the Gospel of Christ?

3. What do you feel is the role of spiritual midwives in the transformation of ministries and the community at large?

4. What daily disciplines do you presently practice to renew your mind? What daily disciplines do you need to adopt or improve?

5. How can believers apply The Midwife Factor in their secular jobs/careers?

8

The Multiplication Factor

*Discipling, Coaching,
and Mentoring Spiritual Midwives*

> *"A person can go to heaven without health, without
> riches, without honors, without learning, without
> friends, but he can never go without Christ."*
>
> **JOHN DYER**

One of the most important factors in sustaining and growing a ministry is succession planning. This is crucial to most secular businesses, and many businesses spend millions of dollars each year to train their employees. Unfortunately, however, we often do not operate with the same wisdom when it comes to Kingdom building. As a result, ministry work can be severely impeded, and some ministries die out completely, due to the lack of able-bodied workers to carry out certain tasks.

When I say "able-bodied" workers, I'm speaking of those who have been *trained* and are *equipped* to carry a ministry forward when the current members are unable to due to declining health, life circumstances, or death. Because let's face it, you can always beg for workers and some, out of the goodness of their hearts, will attempt to assist. However, the problem here is that the majority of "emergency recruits" will most likely lack the specific knowledge needed to make a ministry successful. Acquiring ministry workers when the ministry is in dire need of workers may be necessary, but it's counterproductive because you are forced to "crash-course-train" the workers, sometimes placing too many responsibilities on them at one time which may overwhelm them and cause them not to be faithful to the ministry. Who needs/wants another stressor in his/her life?

As a spiritual midwife, one must disciple, coach, and mentor other spiritual midwives with the same fervor used to help birth a spiritual ministry. Taking on too many roles and not having enough spiritual midwives-in-training puts a strain on the spiritual midwife and on the ministries. You know how we sometimes tend to take on too many responsibilities in ministry and our personal lives (spouses, kids, school activities, work activities, etc.) and then become frustrated with God, life, and everyone else because we are just plain overwhelmed? Well, this can be avoided by properly training others.

We've covered the importance of being able to identify spiritual midwives or those with characteristics of spiritual midwives. These people can be mentored collectively or individually in your church or ministry. But once we identify them, how do we disciple, coach, and mentor them in a way that is fruitful for their personal growth as well as the growth of the ministry and church as a whole? I love the way you ask questions!

The process of discipling, coaching, and mentoring must be viewed as separate engagements that must come together to develop a spiritual midwife for ministry and ministry growth. The key words here are *development* and *growth*. We can view development as continual improvement and growth as multiplication. The business world has these two factors down pat, as most businesses/organizations require ongoing professional development of its employees so that it can continually improve business processes, which leads to earning more money. I don't think anyone is in business to *not* earn money!

What I call the multiplication factor, is called ROI in the financial sector. ROI simply means return on investment. Surely in the Kingdom of God, we should expect a return on our investments as well. Whatever gifts and talents we are given, God expects a return on *His* investment in us! Remember the Parable of the Talents in Matthew 25:14-30? The master left three of His servants in charge while He was away. On

His return, He assessed what His servants had done with the talents He had given them. The first servant, who had been given five talents, had traded them and made another five talents, The second servant, who had received two talents, doubled his also. But the third servant, who had received one talent, hid his talent in the ground—earning nothing. He only gave the master back the one talent he'd been given.

As you might expect, the first two servants were lauded by their master for being faithful with what they'd been given. In fact, he said to them, "Well done my good and faithful servant; you have been faithful over a few things, I will make you ruler over many things. Enter into the joy of your lord." But that third servant, let's just say the master wasn't too pleased with him! The master called him wicked and lazy! Not only that, the third servant's *one* talent was taken away from him and given to the servant who had a total of ten talents! Talk about return on investment! The moral of this story is: whatever gifts, talents, and skills you have, God is expecting *you* to engage in the multiplication factor by producing more fruit and earning him a good return on His investment!

THREE FACTORS OF MULTIPLICATION

Let's talk further about development of the spiritual midwife so we can give God a super ROI! First, we need to understand the three most crucial elements in the multiplication factor: discipleship, coaching, and mentoring. You might be thinking, "What on earth is the difference between discipling, coaching, and mentoring?" I want to define each term so that you understand them as I use or refer to them. Although, I may also use the terms interchangeably, because when developing a spiritual midwife, each term works in concert with the other.

Discipleship is the process by which we help to develop the spiritual aspects of believers. This means helping them to grow in their relationship with God through prayer and studying of the Word, as well as helping them to adequately share the gospel with others, along with their testimony.

Coaching is the process of supporting and encouraging believers in the utilization of their gifts, talents, and skills so that they are productive in ministry. This includes facilitating the sharpening of their gifts, talents, and skills through opportunities to utilize and develop their gifts. In addition, this includes training believers to increase their skill set.

Now, this is radically different from the secular view of coaching where coaching is seen as a means of helping a person identify and achieve their personal goals. There is nothing inherently wrong with creating goals for yourself and achieving them. Our focus, however, in the development of spiritual midwives is to help the spiritual midwives/believers identify their gifts and skills and use them for the glory of God. It's all about multiplication for the Master!

Mentorship is the process of supporting and encouraging believers in their personal lives as they balance family, work, personal goals, challenges, and other relationships. This is the part of the believer that we see, and often the place where the evidence of our spiritual growth or lack thereof shows up! This relationship is valuable to both the mentor and the mentee because both benefit greatly from the interaction. This is normally a long-term relationship that would allow both persons to get to know one another on a deeper level and establish trust so that transparency will be an organic part of the relationship.

The Spiritual Midwife Development Process Framework:

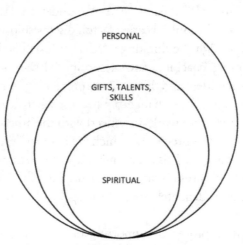

Figure 8.1 The Spiritual MIDWIFE DEVELOPMENT PROCESS Framework

The Spiritual Midwife Development Process framework includes the spiritual self as the catalyst that influences how believers use their gifts, talents, and skills. Both the spiritual realm and the gifts, talents, and skills realm impact believers' personal lives.

MAKING DISCIPLES

The developing of new disciples needs to be done with fidelity and consistency. Close relationships need to be formed between the discipler (one who is engaged in the discipling of another) and the disciple so that proper spiritual growth can occur as well as relational growth. In Matthew 28:19 Jesus calls all Christians to "make disciples of all the nations." As we engage in this general duty as disciples of Christ, we must consider the gifts that lie in those whom we disciple, so that we are able to coach them in the use of their gifts. This is especially true for spiritual midwives. It is imperative that the development of new spiritual midwives be taken seriously as they will serve as supporters of diverse ministries, projects, businesses, programs, etc… that help to further the Kingdom.

For this reason, careful and prayerful consideration needs to be exercised in selecting those who will specifically serve as disciplers/coaches/mentors within the body of the church in one-to-one interactions and small groups. In their book, *The Adventures of Discipling Others: Training in the Art of Disciple Making*, authors Ron Bennett and John Purvis state, "New disciplers need to be willing to commit at least one year to an on-the-job learning process. This means they have or find the freedom in their schedule and responsibilities to give their time and attention to investing in at least one person."[1] Considering that the authors advocate for at least a year of commitment, we can easily note that the process of discipling takes time.

In this instance, we can view time as an opportunity that can allow the discipler and the disciple to establish a relationship of mutual trust and genuine camaraderie, which is essential in building relational ministries. In addition, the discipler-disciple relationship can also be the training ground by which the disciple learns how to connect and build trust. For spiritual midwives, trust building and communication will be the foundational tools needed for their future work in assisting others.

Now, imagine yourself as the discipler. What would this one-year time frame look like for you if you were specifically mentoring newly identified spiritual midwives? How do you see yourself building a genuine relationship with disciples? What methods will you use to build trust? How will you help to strengthen their gifts/talents as spiritual midwives? How will you help to increase their knowledge and application of God's Word so that they are able to share the gospel with confidence (if they are new believers) and learn to lean on the Word as they help "birth" ministries, projects, and the like? These are just some of the questions that need to be incorporated in the training for those who will be discipling/mentoring spiritual midwives.

While discipling focuses on spiritual training and development, as we began to disciple and train spiritual midwives, we must become adept at coaching. Since discipling is our most important call, let's consider that as the foundation of all we do in our work with others. Coaching is another layer on top of that strong foundation. Stay with me, I'm going somewhere with this.

COACHING

We've got our foundation laid. Now it's time to move on to the next layer of building—coaching. This is where we focus on our gift, talent, and skill tools! Earlier I mentioned how businesses routinely engage in succession planning to ensure the continued success of their businesses. Well, we can view coaching as our succession planning in ministry. Here we focus on the spiritual gifts and talents (practical skills) that our disciples/mentees possess.

Those whom we disciple may have a spiritual gift of teaching, administration, or helps. They may be naturally skilled at organization or planning. It's our job as mentors to help sharpen those gifts and talents by training them in various ministry roles and duplicating the process so that they, too, can train the next set of disciples so that the kingdom work gets done no matter what. This is succession planning in a nutshell. We prepare the next group of leaders/workers as we disciple them.

If coaching and succession planning are such good ideas, why isn't it a common practice in our churches? Why do ministries seem to die out? In my interview with Rev. Dr. Kimberly Elyse, a succession planning specialist, she shed light on some of the challenges of succession planning to help understand why it doesn't take place like it should and how we can remedy the problem:

> Some misinterpret the passing of information and seek to take instead of yield. When either the predecessor or the successor is not ready to share or receive instruction, succession can be a frustrating proposition. However, working through this issue and pressing becomes a win for all. There are times when there is an absence on either side (predecessor or successor). In these times it is necessary to seek God for the place of pouring. Who is pouring into? Where is the source of strength? You cannot give from emptiness any more than you can duplicate from a value of "0".[2]

As Rev. Dr. Kimberly Elyse stated, both the predecessor and successor must know their respective roles. It seems that if the discipler views him/herself being pushed out of his/her role, or the disciple isn't ready to be trained, succession or coaching could be problematic.

We can circumvent some succession problems by introducing the concept at the initial ministry planning or the onboarding of a new person on a ministry or project team. This way both coach and the coachee (person being coached) know what to expect. The purpose of coaching needs to be outlined along with the expected outcomes of training each new disciple to be able to duplicate.

Rev. Dr. Elyse also stated that "discipling/coaching is all about teaching people what you have been taught. It's about bringing out of them the gifts that lay inside. When done well it leads them to discipling/coaching others as well."[3] When we look at multiplication/

duplication as the endgame of ministry, it helps us to better develop trainings for our spiritual midwives/coachees. Proper training can incorporate tools necessary to produce desired end-results.

In an interview with Tommye Hinton-Roberts, Principal of Brown ePoints, LLC, a leadership coaching and development firm, she stated that the endgame of the "delivery" in her business is to "inspire leaders to value and exhibit leadership excellence, and that the coachee will identify and understand strengths and weaknesses across three domains of leadership competencies."[4]

Mrs. Hinton-Roberts described her firm's three domains of leadership competencies as follows:

1. Self-awareness

2. Self-mastery

3. A value for excellence in leadership.[5]

These three basic business leadership competencies are ones we should strive to achieve in spiritual leadership. As spiritual midwives, we should also ensure that our coachees strive to achieve them as well. The art of coaching in ministry should always include spiritual excellence. There's doing something right, and then there's doing something with excellence! I have no doubt that God prefers excellence.

Think about when you were in elementary school or higher and you received an A. That felt great, didn't it? Now, think about those times when you knocked it out of the park and your teacher slapped that great big A+ on your paper. Totally different feeling, wasn't it?

Scripture tells us in Colossians 3:23-24, "Work willingly at whatever you do, as though you were working for the Lord rather than for people. Remember that the Lord will give you an inheritance as your reward, and that the Master you are serving is Christ." Ministry work with a pure heart is part of our worship. Coaches and coachees need self-awareness to gauge their progress as well as areas that need to be further developed. Something helpful in training spiritual midwife coaches can be something as simple as Spiritual Midwife Coach and

Coachee self-assessment questionnaires. I've included one of each on the following pages. Feel free to use them and/or create your own as you prepare for multiplication!

SPIRITUAL MIDWIFE COACH
SELF-AWARENESS QUESTIONNAIRE

1. Have you taken a spiritual gifts test? What were the outcomes? Did you have gifts that you weren't aware of?

2. How are you presently utilizing your gifts in ministry?

3. On a scale of 1-10 with one being the lowest and ten being the highest, how would you rate your willingness to disciple/coach/mentor someone on their spiritual journey?

4. In what areas are you most skilled? (For example, organization, writing, event planning, financial planning, record keeping, etc.)

5. How often are you willing to receive ongoing training to improve discipleship, coaching, and mentoring?

6. In what ways will you seek self-improvement in these areas when no training is offered?

7. What do you feel are the most important aspects of serving as a discipler/coach/mentor to another believer?

SPIRITUAL MIDWIFE COACHEE
SELF-AWARENESS QUESTIONNAIRE

1. Have you taken a spiritual gifts test? What were the outcomes? Did you have gifts that you weren't aware of?

2. How are you presently utilizing your gifts in ministry?

3. On a scale of 1-10 with one being the lowest and ten being the highest, how would you rate your willingness to be discipled/mentored/coached by someone as you embark on your journey as a spiritual midwife?

4. In what areas are you most skilled? (For example, organization, writing, event planning, financial planning, record keeping, etc.)

5. In what areas would you like to receive training?

6. What do you feel are your personal weaknesses?

7. In what ways will you seek self-improvement in these areas when no training is offered?

8. How often are you willing to interact with a mentor? What is your preferred method of interaction when you are not able to meet with a mentor in person? (Zoom, phone, text, etc.)

9. What do you hope to gain most from your interaction with a discipler/coach/mentor?

10. What are some important details/character traits about you that would be helpful for your discipler/coach/mentor to know?

11. What are some of the main reasons you want to be discipled/coached/mentored?

MENTORING

To be effective, mentoring needs to be *personal*. Both the mentor/mentee need to be comfortable with one another and there must be transparency in the relationship. Trust is the most important element in the relationship between the mentor and mentee. Life happens, and mentees need to be supported in their personal lives as much as they are supported spiritually. This can be done in practical ways such as assisting a mentee with creating a daily schedule for their home life to alleviate stress or just allowing him/her to vent about their job/work challenges.

Although this relationship is personal, it cannot and should not be forced. The mentor or spiritual midwife must only operate within the level of comfortability the mentee allows. For example, if a spiritual midwife notices that his/her mentee is upset/stressed/overwhelmed, instead of saying, "I've noticed that you seem stressed lately, what's going on?" The mentor can say something like, "I've noticed that you seem stressed lately, how can I assist you?" By responding in this way, the spiritual midwife is not invading his/her mentees privacy or providing unsolicited advice.

TRUST BUILDING IN MENTORING

Trust must be built authentically. Therefore, the spiritual midwife who is doing the mentoring must become a great listener without always offering solutions. In fact, until a level of comfortability and trust is established on both ends, it is always better to ask before offering solutions. Some believe mentors/coaches should not give advice. I'm not in that camp because I believe that people who are being mentored and coached sometimes need advice when they are unsure how to respond to certain life situations. However, it's best to pose possible solutions as questions until the mentee is in a comfortable enough emotional trusting space to receive advice/solutions from his/her mentor. For example, before sharing possible solutions/advice a mentor can say something like, "Have you considered…???" Also, a spiritual midwife who has established a trusting relationship may offer something like, "When I dealt with a similar situation, I found the following to be helpful…" This allows the spiritual midwife to share without telling the mentee what he/she should do. Most importantly, even when sharing practical advice, the word of God should serve as the foundation for solutions.

A spiritual midwife must not rush the mentoring process, but instead allow the relationship to blossom naturally through the sharing of common interests, praying, and sharing of the Word. The mentor/mentee relationship reminds me of a story someone emailed me by an unknown author, titled, "I Love You Enough… Not to Let Go."

> Some years ago, on a hot summer day in south Florida, a little boy decided to go for a swim in the old swimming hole behind his house. In a hurry to dive into the cool water, he ran out the back door, leaving behind shoes, socks, and shirt as he went.
>
> He flew into the water, not realizing that as he swam toward the middle of the lake, an alligator was swimming toward the shore.
>
> His father working in the yard saw the two as they got closer and closer together. In utter fear, he ran toward the water, yelling to his son as loudly as he could.
>
> Hearing his voice, the little boy became alarmed and made a U-turn to swim to his father. It was too late. Just as he reached his father, the alligator reached him. From the dock, the father grabbed his little boy by the arms just as the alligator snatched his legs. That began an incredible tug-of-war between the two. The alligator was much stronger than the father, but the father was much too passionate to let go. A farmer happened to drive by, heard his screams, raced from his truck, took aim, and shot the alligator.
>
> Remarkably, after weeks and weeks in the hospital, the little boy survived. His legs were extremely scarred by the vicious attack of the animal. And, on his arms, were deep

scratches where his father's fingernails dug into his flesh in his effort to hang on to the son he loved.

The newspaper reporter, who interviewed the boy after the trauma, asked if he would show him his scars. The boy lifted his pant legs. And then, with obvious pride, he said to the reporter, "But look at my arms. I have great scars on my arms, too. I have them because my Dad wouldn't let go." [6]

SUPPORTING A MENTEE EMOTIONALLY

Perhaps you can connect and relate to the excitement of the scars made from the boy's dad in the "I Love You Enough… Not to Let Go" story. Many of us display scars made through struggles that occurred at various points in our lives. No, maybe not from an alligator, but scars of painful past experiences or even from spiritual battles. Birthing scars showing where "new" birth or opportunity for "new" birth was to result. You didn't perish. God saw your struggle and positioned someone to take hold of you and not let go. Despite the resistance from the outside, from you, or from within, this appointed person didn't let go. Certainly, God had you!!!

Scars are unsightly and at times draw unwanted attention. Some have caused us sorrow and deep regret. We must realize, as the son did in the story, that some wounds are the result of our faithful and loving God refusing to let us go.

He has been present holding onto us, often providing for us through others. In the midst of the struggles we have encountered, He has not released us. He has a hold on us. This is the message and advice we as spiritual midwives can readily share with our mentees or other spiritual midwives.

God loves you. You are His child. In Jeremiah 29:11, The Lord says, "For I know the plans I have for you. They are plans for good and not for disaster, to give you a future and a hope." He is ready and able to protect you and provide for you. However, at times, we foolishly wander into or blatantly place ourselves in dangerous situations, not knowing or thinking about what is up ahead.

Life's swimming hole is filled with dangers and peril—there is an enemy waiting to steal, kill, and destroy. He is waiting for an opportunity to prevent you from delivering all that God has called, positioned, anointed, gifted, and designed you to be. The enemy comes in various forms to get you to abort. He even solicits your help to fear or operate in unbelief and self-doubt so you will quit and not pursue the plans God has for you.

I believe that in the spiritual realm there is a tug-of-war going on over you and you often bear the scars of that struggle. These spiritual scars are similar to the physical scars the son in the story suffered, proving his father did not let go, just as your Father does not let go. If you have the scars of His love on your arms, be very, very grateful. He did not and will not *ever* let you go.

As we go about our daily duties, we often forget that the enemy is waiting to attack. That's when the tug-of-war begins. We never know exactly where a person is on his/her spiritual journey or what they are going through. As God gives you discernment as a spiritual midwife to see the battle scars of another person's past that may be holding them hostage, pray that He gives you the strength to apply the Midwife Factor as they focus on their present while preparing for the glorious future God has in store for them.

THE MIDWIFE FACTOR MEDITATION

- *We must engage in succession planning in order to ensure the continuity of our ministries.*

- *God expects a return on His investment, so we must multiply our gifts talents and skills!*

- *When serving as a spiritual midwife who is a discipler/coach/ mentor we must remember to address the spiritual aspect of our mentees, their gifts, talents, and skills, as well as their personal interests and concerns.*

THE MIDWIFE FACTOR
ESSENTIAL CARE REFLECTION

1. Who are the characters in your life (father, son, farmer, or alligator)?

2. Who has been assigned to your life (as the farmer in the story) to be a spiritual midwife, operating as His birthing assistant to the goals/visions/dreams God has given you?

3. Who or what has been the alligator that's pulling on you preventing or trying to prevent you from being all that God has called you to be?

4. Who is the one in your life who won't let go and has held onto you even though it hurts and left birthing scars on you and/or them?

5. What are some ways they didn't let go?

6. In your journey, what are some of the birthing scars that remain from your deliverance?

7. What are the scars that have healed?*

---

* If you have scars that have not healed, please pray God will help you to forgive and apply EGR (Extra Grace Required) where needed to bring wholeness in you.

9

Testimony

The Birthing of a Spiritual Midwife

> *"God has always used ordinary people to carry out His extraordinary missions."*
>
> **CAROL KENT**

Some years ago, I was asked to share a personal testimony at church during the week of Advent—the birthing season. As you may already know, giving a testimony is indeed invasive, speaking publicly about personal issues you may not want more than a few close people in your life to know.

As I was moved to share my story, I looked out and saw some unfamiliar faces and was immediately reminded of the Word of God in the first portion of Revelation 12:11, *KJV*, "And they overcame him by the blood of the Lamb, and by the word of their testimony…"

I'm asking you now to consider the following two questions I asked the congregation that night:

1. Could it be we don't experience the overcoming power that is available to us because we fail to give the word of our own testimonies?

2. Is your ability to overcome that struggle you are currently in hidden behind a set of lips?

As you ponder these questions, I am going to share my testimony with you. It is the story of my physical birth and the transformation that took place to birth me anew! More specifically, it's His story in my life!

INSIDE JOB

My new birth was an inside job, in which God had already set the parameters. The Word says in Jeremiah 29:11, "For I know the plans I have for you," says the Lord. "They are plans for good and not for disaster, to give you a future and a hope." I was delivered from my mother's womb into sin and surrounded by sin. My mother chose to endure the stigma attached to having a child out of wedlock in the late 40's. I offer up thanks to God that my mother chose not to abort me but instead made the decision to keep, love, and train me outside of a covenant of marriage with my natural father. I appreciate her for permitting me to *be*. I was almost 13 years old before I even found out about the circumstances surrounding my birth.

As the time for my mother to deliver me drew near, my cousin Elsie, a midwife, traveled from New Jersey to Detroit, Michigan to assist with my birth. Although my mother and biological father never married, he provided support and provisions for my care at a distance, as my mother proceeded with her life. My mother soon married a man who became my "Daddy" and her husband until his death separated them after over 40 years of marriage.

Like a caterpillar that eventually finds itself in a cocoon, I too found myself cocooned as life happened. I thank God for having been taught about His Son as far back as I can remember. My recollection of my first reading lessons was on my Big Ma's knee, as she instructed me how to read the Word of God. Because of her, I was able to invite Jesus into my heart at an early age. This decision started the inside job, even though on the outside of the cocoon many things were being formed that could have led to my destruction. But God's plan for good, a future and a hope were developing within me, and I thank Him for that! I have the PROMISES of God, PEACE of Jesus and POWER of the Holy Spirit!

WEAPONRY

Outside the cocoon, however, brutal and destructive weapons were being formed as I matured into womanhood. During my marriage, demons made themselves at home where my family and I lived. I Thank God for pulling down strongholds and the spiritual exterminators He sent to instruct me concerning cleaning my house and filling my home with His Holy Spirit during that time. Then a deep depression encompassed one of my children, which led to a suicide attempt. The resulting ordeal lasted for three months before God delivered us out of that darkness. I give thanks to a DELIVERING God. Soon after, devastating disease was launched toward one of my children with what appeared to be spinal meningitis. Then yet another child suffered from repeated heart and breathing problems. And yet, God healed!

I faced unfathomable deception after 23 years of marriage when I discovered a notation by my husband indicating that he had wanted to leave me after the first three years of marriage but was "not in position to leave." Can you imagine finding a notation by your husband stating he wanted out of the marriage?

A year prior to my husband deserting me, he had been "wrongfully" dismissed from his job. That same year, our oldest child graduated from high school and entered college. After five months of my husband being unemployed, the Lord told me to encourage him to pursue the matter of his dismissal, and that his position and wages would be totally restored to him.

The matter was pursued with the help of his labor union representative, and over a year later, my husband accepted a settlement that only cost him two weeks of pay. He was restored to his position and returned to work. Two months after he returned to work, he received the settlement check for all his missed wages minus two weeks of pay. A month later, he had moved in with the union representative.

Two months after my husband left, I awoke at 2:30 AM. I was directed by the Lord to box up the last of his belongings. Among his textbooks was a sociology book from a class he had taken. It happened to be the last book I placed in the box. As I placed it in the box, I was directed by the Lord to "open this one." The notation in the margin of the book had been made early in our marriage. It was in reference to the example of a married couple where the husband did not have the financial resources to get out of the marriage, so he stayed. My husband's notation was: "This is my situation; I am not in position to leave." He had stayed with me for twenty years until he finally felt he was in position to move on—until he felt he could act on his desire.

He filed to divorce me a few months later and many strange events followed in and out of our legal system. I thank God for ministering to me and separating the wheat from the tare, sharing that no part of me was torn or damaged in His separation. I also give thanks to God for being a God of Justice; for His Word, in 1 Corinthians 7:15 that says, if he leaves let him go. I also thank God for allowing me to come to know the "peace that passes all understanding."

My son and I experienced division during this difficult time, and sadly there was division between my son and his sisters as well. The relationships were extremely hard to navigate after the divorce. I thank God for being a God of reconciliation and I trusted Him for restoration, for unity and for redeeming the time.

Wouldn't you know after all of that, just a few years later, my kidneys were attacked causing me to have three major surgeries on my kidneys within a five-day period! I thank God for His healing power, His provisions, His keeping power, His promises, and His Word. You do know that "no weapon formed against you will succeed…" (Isaiah 54:17, *HCSB*). The Word doesn't say no weapon will be formed. It just promises it won't succeed.

You see the enemy has tried so hard to eliminate me through his attempts of destruction—destroying my marriage, and attacking my children and me. I thank God for the plans He has for me that are of good and not evil and truly for redeeming my life from the destruction (see Psalms 103:3-4, *KJV*).

NEW BIRTH

I thank God for His grace to forgive, His promise to never leave me, His strength and wisdom, and for His invitation for me to *just trust* Him, so I could experience "walking by faith and not by sight." Believing what He told me, that God Himself caused my husband to leave because he would not turn. I also give thanks to God for His provisions, and I have come to understand that His grace *is* sufficient. During the time of my divorce, my daughter was awarded a full academic scholarship with a paying summer internship for four years. Through the Lord's guidance, I was able to maintain our family lifestyle with very little adjustments. I experienced no repossessions or utility cutoffs. Praise God!

Through the grace of God, I chose to forgive all those who were used by Satan. I prayed for their salvation, enlightenment, and deliverance. I asked the Lord to bless them and to send them laborers that would help them to know His Son, Jesus Christ, and accept Him as their Lord and Savior.

I give thanks to God who revealed the parameters for my new life in Him and gave me opportunities to grow in Him through the struggles of the breaking out of the cocoon that engulfed me. Death. Yes, the death of Audrey was needed for a new birth! Because of my willingness to forgive others and their willingness to forgive me, God's grace, mercy, and favor, has allowed my family to redeem the time and experience restoration and reconciliation in our relationships. Through developing, growing, and being fed through the umbilical cord of the Heavenly Father, I stand with an attitude of thanksgiving for I have experienced yet another deliverance which brought me into my new birth.

Most of all, I thank God for eternal life through His Son Jesus the Christ!

THE MIDWIFE FACTOR MEDITATION

- *Your personal testimony is a witness to what God has done for you and what he can do for others!*

- *The Lord is with you during every step of your life, even in the dark times when you feel the most beat up and defeated.*

- *With God's strength you can endure and overcome life's challenges.*

- *God will use your experiences to create a new you.*

THE MIDWIFE FACTOR
PERSONAL TESTIMONY REFLECTION

1. What is your method for sharing your personal testimony with others?

2. What tragic/disappointing situations or experiences have God brought you through that may bless and strengthen someone else?

3. What scriptures do you meditate on when you experience difficult situations in life?

4. How have you grown spiritually as a result of the challenges you have experienced?

ACKNOWLEDGEMENTS

I thank God for my grandmother Big Ma, my Mama, Daddy, Pa Lenyoun, Pa & Ma Tolliver, Ma Blackburn, Mama D, Grace M., Gwen H., Rev. Story, and Rev. Dr. Frederick G. Sampson (*All have gone home to be with our Lord.*). These were Spiritual Midwives that God enabled to assist in my development and birthing process. I ask for continued prayer for me as I continue to grow in the Lord.

God has been faithful to position additional individuals, more than I can list, to function as spiritual midwives in my continued growth. I thank God for my Pastor of the last seventeen years, Rev. Dr. Nathan Johnson, who has and currently provides a spiritual covering for me as I serve using my spiritual gifts in ministry. Additionally, I thank him for the wisdom he shares continually. Pastor Johnson reminded us that "God specializes in creating something from nothing and that God has options we don't have." I can certainly look back and give testimony to both of these truths.

I also am thankful for the morning I was awakened to the Lord telling me, "It's time. The spiritual midwife needs a spiritual midwife." Upon my suggesting a name, God told me "no" and said, "Sherrhonda Denice." She is to be my Spiritual Midwife to get this book birthed. By the way, it's been developing for three decades. I am grateful.

I thank my children who have blessed me beyond belief: Kimberly Elyse; Otis Kinard (Maria) McGresham; Kristan (Adrian) Marshall. I am especially awed by the spiritual legacy that God is building through my grandchildren: Dorian Walker, Keziah Kudowor, Moriyah Marshall, Sophia McGresham, Amani Marshall, and Ariana Marshall. What great blessings!

Appendix: 1

Scripture Resources

LET THE WORD OF GOD
DEFINE YOUR NEW BIRTH

1. Your partnership with Christ (Isaiah 61:1-3)

2. The process to follow Christ (Ephesians 4:1-3)

3. Your position in Christ (Ephesians 4:11)

4. Your participation in the body of Christ
   (Ephesians 4:12-13)

5. Your patience in the race as you look to Christ
   (Hebrews 12:1-2)

6. The product produced when you go in Christ
   (Matthew 28:19-20)

7. Your peace through Christ (Philippians 4:7)

*You must keep in focus that it is
ALL FOR THE GLORY OF GOD!*

Notes

CHAPTER 1

1. *Merriam-Websters Dictionary* "midwife," accessed August 13, 2021, https://www.merriam-webster.com/dictionary/midwife.

2. Margaret Guenther, "A Spiritual Midwife: God's Helpers in Birthing New Life," accessed August 19, 2021, https://www.rodwhite.net/tag/margaret-guenther/.

3. Gillis Triplett, "Honorable Men Seek Spiritual Midwives," accessed August 19, 2021, https://www.gillistriplett.com/rel101/articles/wives.html.

CHAPTER 2

1. Rev. Dr. Nathan Johnson, "The Resiliency of the Righteous," (unpublished) June 16, 2021.

2. J. Christopher Mc Michael, "Helps Ministry Lesson 1: Introduction to Helps," accessed August 11, 2021, https://podschool.org/wp-content/uploads/2018/02/HELPS-MINISTRY-PT_1-Pod-School-Lesson-020218.pdf.

3. "Helps: What is it?," Compelling Truth. Author unknown accessed August 11, 2021, https://www.compellingtruth.org/gift-of-helps.html.

4. J. Christopher McMichael, "Helps Ministry Lesson 1: Introduction to Helps."

5. J. Christopher Mc Michael, "Helps Ministry Lesson 1: Introduction to Helps."

6. Sherrhonda Denice, Interviewed by Audrey McGresham, Redford, MI, August 5, 2021.

7. Chere Nabor, Interviewed by Audrey McGresham, Redford, MI, July 13, 2021.

8. Ibid.

9. Alison Doyle, "What are Soft Skills? Definitions and Examples," The Balance Careers, accessed August 17, 2021, https://www.thebalancecareers.com/what-are-soft-skills-2060852.

CHAPTER 3

1. Hein van Wyk, "Ministry Leadership Fails: Six Reasons Why," accessed August 20, 2021, https://www.sharefaith.com/blog/2016/05/ministry-leadership-fails-six-reasons/.

CHAPTER 4

1. Kristan Marshall, interviewed by Audrey McGresham, Redford, MI, July 14, 2021.

2. Orlando Arnold, interviewed by Audrey McGresham, Redford, MI, July 28, 2021.

3. Quentin Goins, interviewed by Audrey McGresham, Redford, MI, August 8, 2021.

CHAPTER 6

1. Merriam Webster's Dictionary, "barrenness," accessed August 21, 2021, https://www.merriam-webster.com/dictionary/barren.

CHAPTER 7

1. Gary C. Newton, *Heart-Deep Teaching: Engaging Students for Transformed Lives* (Nashville, Tennessee: B & H Academic, 2012), 13.
2. Teresa of Avila "Christ Has No Body," accessed August 3, 2021, https://www.Journeywithjesus.net.
3. Dr. Otis McGresham, interviewed by Audrey McGresham, Redford, MI, July 21, 2021.

CHAPTER 8

1. Ron Bennett and John Purvis, *The Adventure of Discipling Others: Training in the Art of Disciplemaking* (Colorado Springs, CO.: NavPress, 2003), 11.
2. Rev. Dr. Kimberly Elyse, interview by Audrey McGresham, Redford, MI, May 6, 2021.
3. Ibid
4. Tommye Hinton-Roberts, interview by Audrey McGresham, Redford, MI, July 9, 2021.
5. Ibid.
6. Anonymous, "I Love You Enough... Not to Let Go." Personal email accessed November 8, 2005.